THE F
SHOP GUIDE

© **Copyright** *Gillian Cutress.*
All rights reserved.
Material in this book is copyright but may be used by a purchaser for his/ her own reference. It may not be used as a basis for selling direct mail services to others, nor may copies of the whole or part be made for any purpose whatsoever by any form of copying process, including data processing systems, without the prior written consent and agreement of the copyright holder, Gillian Cutress. The owner of the copyright has the exclusive right to make copies. No part of this book may be used for compiling another list or directory. Information may not be copied from this copyright work and sent out, for confirmation or correction.

ISBN 0 948965 57 6

ISSN 0969–4994

THE FACTORY SHOP GUIDE

East Anglia & South-East England

- ✔ Where they are
- ✔ When they open
- ✔ What they sell
- ✔ How to get there

Published by
Gillian Cutress
and Rolf Stricker

Personally researched, written & published by:
Gillian Cutress & Rolf Stricker
1 Rosebery Mews, Rosebery Road,
London SW2 4DQ
Phone 0181-678 0593
Fax 0181-674 1594

1991 *The Factory Shop Guide: East Anglia & Sout-East England 1991–92*
1992 *The Factory Shop Guide: East Anglia & Sout-East England 1992–93*
1993 *The Factory Shop Guide: East Anglia & Sout-East England 1993–94*
1995 *The Factory Shop Guide: East Anglia & Sout-East England 1995–96*

This is the 57th edition published in this series

Changes and Mistakes

When possible, entries in this Guide were checked by the companies just before we went to press. But – especially so in the current economic climate – organisations change, shops open at new times, holidays alter, shops decide to close for stocktaking and, from time to time, a shop ceases trading. We regret any inconvenience such changes cause, but these things do happen.

Therefore we cannot recommend strongly enough that you should phone first if you are going a long way or are making a special journey.

We have done our best to ensure that all the information in this Guide is correct. However, as we deal with thousands of details, it is possible that an error has occasionally slipped in. Do please let us know of any such slip you notice. As every reasonable care has been taken in the preparation of this book, we can accept no responsibility for errors, omissions, or damage, however caused.

CONTENTS

Introduction	7
Size chart	8
Details about factory shops	9–79
Information about other money-saving guide books	88–92
Order form	94
Comments on factory shops Would you like a free book next year? What do you look for in a factory shop?	95–96
Market days	97
List of towns with factory shops	98–99
List of companies with factory shops	100–101
Index	102–104

Maps can be found on the following pages

High Wycombe	36
Ipswich	37
King's Lynn	40
London	47
South London	57
Norwich	61
South-East England	80
Hampshire area	81
Surrey/Sussex/Kent	82–83
Herts/Essex/Suffolk	84–85
East Anglia	86–87

The Factory Shop Guide for East Anglia & South-East England

A selection of factory shops in East Anglia & South-East England

ADD INTEREST AND FUN TO YOUR SHOPPING AND SAVE TIME AND MONEY INTO THE BARGAIN!

Welcome

Factory shopping makes a day out with a difference! If you have not yet discovered this enticing new world, don't delay. This book tells you how, when and where to find excellent value shopping by going directly to the manufacturer.

Rapidly gaining a much higher profile in East Anglia, the home counties and South-East England, factory shopping offers an ever wider choice. You can either visit the mill or factory and have pleasure in buying from the maker on site or, to an increasing extent, you can buy a selection of different manufacturers' products from one location. Merchants Quay in Brighton, with a variety of factory shops beside the yacht marina, opened as we published this book; other centres are planned for East Anglia and elsewhere in the south. The principle is the same: the shops sell off manufacturers' overmakes, excess stock and ends of lines; the public benefits by finding excellent value for money.

In other shops you find top value by going to the maker, thus cutting out the middle man. Some of the outlets described belong to companies who have special links with a particular manufacturer, thereby getting very good deals.

Many people new to factory shops made the mistaken assumption that such shops supply just clothes. Nothing could be further from the truth! A quick glance at the index at the back of this guide shows that you can buy an extraordinary range of items for the home and for the garden, as well as to wear. Everthing we have bought for the last ten years – from garden pots to carpets, cutlery, cruets and cashmere – started life in a factory shop.

Because we have ourselves spent so many hours on the road searching out these shops, we try to give detailed and accurate instructions on how to find them. We recognize that people want to spend their time shopping, not looking for the shops! To help you relax while looking for bargains, we add extra details about parking your car and where to get a cup of tea.

The aim of this book is to help you enhance your life-style at a much lower cost than you expect. At times of recession (and we do not seem to have seen the end of it yet!), looking for top value becomes even more important. Enjoy your shopping while finding the finer things in life for less!

Gill and Rolf

> Sincere thanks go to Emma,
> who has put much effort into compiling this book.

"Just bought your marvellous book last week and I love the mentality that even though I may spend a lot, I'm saving even more. My husband is not too sure about this at the moment, especially as we've just bought a new house and need so many things..." Mrs GT, Flitwick

The Factory Shop Guide for East Anglia & South-East England

SIZE CHART

With this chart you have no excuse for not knowing the sizes of your family or your home!

NAME										
Ring size										
Shoes										
Socks										
Tights Stockings										
Pants										
Bra										
Shirt collar										
Jacket										
Trouser leg										
Trouser waist										
Trousers										
Sweater										
Skirt										
Dress Blouse										
Bust Waist Hip										

ROOM										
Bed size										
Yds fabric upholstery										
Rolls wallpaper										
Yds fabric needed 2										
Curtain length 2										
Window width 2										
Yds fabric needed 1										
Curtain length 1										
Window width 1										
Room Size										

The Factory Shop Guide for East Anglia & South-East England

1 Arundel W Sussex

The Factory Shop

8 Castle Mews, Tarrant Street BN18 9DF
(01903) 883797

Golfwear for ladies and gents including plus-twos and knickerbockers; sweaters and trousers.
Leisurewear for ladies and gents including sweatshirts, joggers, knitwear, skirts and trousers.
'Ends of lines (no seconds) from factories supplying major high street chains, and golf clubs at up to 50% off normal prices.'

....

In the centre of town.
   From Worthing via A27: go over river into town, follow one-way system into High Street. Pass memorial on right. Take next left, Tarrant Street (opposite Norfolk Arms Hotel).*
   From Chichester via A27: at large roundabout, go left for Town Centre. Go into one-way system – you come to castle walls. Go downhill; 20 yds after yellow brick NatWest bank on right, go right, Tarrant Street.*
   *Shop 150 yds on right, set back at rear of cobbled mews.

Open: Tues–Sat 9.30–5.30; Sun and Bank Holidays 11–5.
Closed: Monday; Christmas, Boxing and New Year's Days.
Cards: Access, Amex, Delta, Eurocard, Mastercard, Switch, Visa.
Cars: Free 1-hr parking in Tarrant St; local car-parks.
Toilets: Yes.
Wheelchairs: Two steps to medium sized shop.
Changing rooms: Yes.
Teas: Many local tea-shops.
Groups: Shoppers welcome; please phone Mr Macro first.
Transport: Any bus or train to Arundel.

2 Aylesbury Bucks

The Chiltern Brewery

Nash Lee Road, Terrick HP17 0TO
(01296) 613647

Beer brewed here including de-luxe Old Ale (pint bottles) & barley wine (1/2 pints). Unique range of beer-related items – beer and mustard cheeses, mild and strong beer mustards, Old Ale chutney, malt marmalade, barley wine cake, onions pickled in hop vinegar, pickled eggs and some pickled customers! New range of beer, malt and hop-based toiletries, eg shampoo. Books, beer recipes. Hampers; fruit wines, speciality ciders.

'Most people regard the brewery as an experience to visit, not just a shopping excursion. Ask for leaflet, mentioning this book.'

....

Village 4 miles south of Aylesbury, 2 1/2 miles west of Wendover.
   From A413 (Aylesbury–Wendover road): go west on to B4009 for Princes Risborough/High Wycombe. Keep going for just under a mile; brewery well signposted on left, in farm building.
   From Princes Risborough: take A4010 north for Aylesbury. After Great Kimble go right at next roundabout, following signs to Wendover (B4009). Keep straight; brewery short distance on right.

Open: Mon–Sat 9–5; Bank Holidays.
Closed: Christmas, Boxing and New Year's Days.
Cards: No.
Cars: Own yard.
Toilets: Yes.
Wheelchairs: No steps.
Teas: In Aylesbury and Wendover.
Tours: For 12–50 people by arrangement during the day: Tippler's tour, £5.50, includes a free drink, as does the Drayman's at £9.95 (including substantial buffet). Also self-conducted tours, £1 per head, and regular Saturday tours, £2.50 each, at 12 noon, by Head Brewer. England's first small brewery museum now included in tours.
Transport: Aylesbury–High Wycombe buses stop 1/4 mile away.

The Factory Shop Guide for East Anglia & South-East England

3 Aylsham Norfolk
Black Sheep Ltd.
9 Penfold Street NR11 6ES
(01263) 733142

Knitwear and classic country wear for men, women and children in pure oiled wool of Black Welsh sheep; gifts and accessories.

'Undyed wool comes from local flock of sheep which you may see in Ingworth, further north. Most items perfect but always some seconds. Mail-order catalogue – please mention this book when requesting it.'

....

100 yds from the Market Place in Aylsham, near the post office.
  Leave Market Place with Black Boys Inn on your right (going towards Reepham and Blickling (B1354/B1145); pass post office on left – shop is 100 yds on left, clearly visible.
  From Cawston (B1145) or Blickling (B1354): look for old pump, with columns and thatched roof, where these two roads meet at start of town. Shop is opposite this pump, on right corner as you go into village.

Open: Mon–Sat 9–5.30.
Closed: Bank Holidays; Christmas and Boxing Days.
Cards: Access, Amex, Visa.
Cars: Limited parking beside shop; local streets.
Toilets: In village.
Wheelchairs: Easy access, medium-sized shop (steps to rear area).
Changing rooms: Yes.
Teas: Pubs in village.
Groups: You can see knitwear being made in next building but no demonstrations. Shopping groups with prior notice.
Transport: Any bus to Aylsham.

4 Barkingside Essex
Choice Discount Stores Ltd.
26–28 High Street IG6 2DO
(0181) 551 2125

Surplus stocks including men's, women's and children's fashions from *Next plc*, *Next Directory* and other high street fashions. *Next Interiors* and footwear.

'Save up to 50% of normal Next first quality prices; seconds sold from 1/3 of normal retail price. Special sales Jan and Sept.'

....

In modern dark brown building in the High Street.
  From the south on A123 from Gants Hill roundabout: pass the Barkingside police station and McDonald's on left and Chequers pub on right. The shop is about 100 yds on right in the only brown building.
  From the north and Fullwell Cross on A123: pass the Fullwell Cross swimming pool and recreation centre on left, go across pedestrian lights and the shop is 100 yds on left after the next street traffic lights.

Open: Mon–Sat 9–5.30; Sun 10–4.
Closed: Easter Sunday; Christmas and Boxing Days.
Cards: Access, Amex, Switch, Visa.
Cars: In street or in Sainsbury's large car-park.
Toilets: No.
Wheelchairs: No steps to large shop.
Changing rooms: No, but refund if returned in perfect condition within 28 days.
Teas: In town centre.
Groups: Shopping groups welcome! Book with store manager.
Transport: Gants Hill tube station, then bus nos. 129, 150 or 167. Barkingside tube station, then a short walk.
Mail order: No.

5 Basildon Essex
Choice Discount Stores Ltd.

*Unit 6a, Mayflower Retail Park, Gardiners Link SS14 3AR
(01268) 288331*

Surplus stocks including men's, women's and children's fashions from *Next plc, Next Directory* and other high street fashions. *Next Interiors* and footwear.

'Save up to 50% of normal Next first quality prices; seconds sold from 1/3 of normal retail price. Special sales Jan and Sept.'

....

North-east of Basildon, next to huge Tesco and Pizza Hut.
   From London on A127: don't turn off onto A176 but take next exit for A132 and turn back on yourself towards London on A127.*
   From the east on A127: pass over the exit for A132, continuing straight.*
   From Basildon centre: follow signs to Wickford A132. Pass the huge Watermill pub on right, then GEC Marconi Avionics on left and then turn onto A127 towards London.*
   *After 800 yds take slip road signposted to Mayflower Retail Park. Pass McDonald's on left and shop is near the end next to Pizza Hut.

Open: Mon, Tues, Wed 9–6; Thur, Fri 9–7; Sat 9–5.30; Sun 11–5.
Closed: Easter Sunday; Christmas and Boxing Days.
Cards: Access, Amex, Switch, Visa.
Cars: Large free car-park in front of store.
Toilets: At Tesco nearby.
Wheelchairs: Easy access. No steps.
Changing rooms: No, but refunds if returned in perfect condition within 28 days.
Teas: On-site Tesco, McDonald's, Kentucky.
Groups: Shopping groups welcome! Book with store manager.
Transport: Wickford BR station or Basildon BR station.
Mail order: No.

6 Basildon Essex
The Factory Shop

*4c The Gloucesters, Luckyn Lane, Pipps Hill Industrial Estate
SS14 3AY   (01268) 520446*

Large selection of melamine, household lines, china, glass, linens, fancy goods, toys, garden furniture and accessories, seasonal lines and novelties, greetings and Christmas cards, paper, stationery. Underwear, clothes, tracksuits, trainers and some food.

'Specialise in ends of ranges: brand name stock clearances, seconds, rejects, ends of line etc.'

....

On Industrial Estate north-east of Basildon.
   From M25 exit 29: take A127 for Southend. Look for A176 Basildon/Billericay exit – at end of slip road go left; take first left, Miles Gray Rd. At traffic lights go right; take 1st left, Luckyn Lane.*
   Going towards London on A127: take A176 (Basildon/Billericay exit). At end of slip road, go straight across on to Miles Gray Road. At traffic lights, go right. Take first left (Luckyn Lane).*
   *Shop clearly signed on right.
   From town centre: take A176 for Billericay. At large roundabout, go right for Pipps Hill; at next roundabout go left; take first left, Luckyn Lane; shop 200 yds on left.

Open: Mon–Sat 9–5.30; Sun and Bank Holidays 10–5.
Closed: Christmas and Boxing Days.
Cards: Access, Amex, Switch, Visa.
Cars: Outside shop.
Toilets: Ask if desperate.
Wheelchairs: Easy access, no steps to huge shop.
Changing rooms: Yes.
Teas: Cold drinks, prepacked sandwiches, crisps and sweets.
Groups: Groups welcome to shop, but please phone Mr Cantor first.
Mail order: No.

The Factory Shop Guide for East Anglia & South-East England

7 Basingstoke Hants
Western House Ltd.
Armstrong Road, Daneshill Estate RG24 8QF
(01256) 462341

Large selection of glassware, cookware, oven-to-tableware and ceramics; silverware; giftware.

'Well established distributor of glassware, gifts, ceramics at factory prices. Arrange glass engraving. First and second class qualities available.'

....

On east side of Basingstoke 2 miles from town centre.
  From M3 exit 6: follow sign for A33 towards Reading/Daneshill Ind. Est.*
  From town centre, follow signs to Reading.*
  *At Reading Road roundabout (second roundabout off M3) follow signs to Daneshill Ind. Est.; go left into Faraday Road. Follow this road round to Daneshill roundabout; go straight over into Swing Swang Lane. Armstrong Road is first road on right; company clearly visible along on left.

Open: Tues–Fri 10–4; Sat 9–2.
Closed: Bank Holidays; Christmas, Boxing and New Year's Days.
Cards: Access, Visa.
Cars: Car-park in front of shop.
Toilets: No.
Wheelchairs: No steps to very large ground floor shop on one level.
Teas: Basingstoke.
Groups: No.
Transport: Local buses along Swing Swang Lane.
Mail order: Yes. No seconds sent.
Catalogue: No.

8 Beaconsfield Bucks
The Curtain Shuffle
Unit 3, 194 Maxwell Road HP9 1QY
(01494) 680662

Huge range of new curtains which are ends of line, slight substandards, overmakes, cancelled orders etc. Cushions, tie backs, bedheads. Also secondhand curtains sold on commission.

....

Coming along the M40, exit at Junction 2.
  Coming north on the A355: go into old Beaconsfield and at roundabout in town, go right on the B474 for Beaconsfield New Town, Penn and Hazlemere. As you reach the shops, go over the pedestrian lights and take the first right (Maxwell Road) in front of WH Smith. After 10 yds go left into the yard for the well-marked shop.
  Coming into town from Penn on the B474: go over the railway, straight at the two mini-roundabouts, then left into Maxwell Road immediately after WH Smith.

Open: Tues–Sat 9.30-4.30.
Closed: Bank Holidays; Christmas–New Year.
Cards: No.
Cars: In yard, or side roads.
Toilets: In town.
Wheelchairs: One step to medium-sized shop.
Teas: In main street.
Groups: Not suitable for shopping groups.
Transport: Any bus or train to Beaconsfield.

9 Beccles Suffolk

Winter Flora
Hall Farm, Weston NR34 8TT      (01502) 713346

Locally grown flowers & grasses; dried flower arrangements. Fine selection of silk flowers; foliage from Italy and South Africa; exotics from South Africa, Brazil and India; moss from Iceland; baskets from Philippines and China; copper bowls from Turkey; ceramics from Spain; glass from Egypt. Ribbons, foam, clay, wires, glue, sundries for flower arrangements.

'Commissions taken for bridal and special occasions; also garlands and swags.'

....

Beccles is 8 miles inland from Lowestoft, on the A146. Weston is 1 mile south of Beccles centre.

From main roads on north side of town: follow signs into Beccles. Go over bridge and into one-way system; cross traffic lights. At T-junction go left (don't go towards town centre). Pass Esso on right, immediately turn right into Peddars Lane. Take first left (London Rd) and keep going for 3/4 mile; pass industrial estate on left. Winter Flora clearly marked on right; go down long drive.

From the south: turn off the A12 just beyond Blythburgh and take the A145 for Beccles; go through Weston – Winter Flora clearly marked on left.

Open: *Jan–Mar* daily 10–3.30; *Apr–Dec* daily 10–5.
Closed: 24–29 December.
Cards: Access, Visa.
Cars: Large car-park
Toilets: Yes.
Wheelchairs: One step to workshop and shop.
Teas: In Beccles.
Groups: Welcome at English Flower Farm at Weston where you can see traditional and inspirational arrangements being made in workshop. Please phone first.
Transport: Trains to Beccles then taxi.
Mail order: No.

10 Bedford Beds

Boynett Fabrics Factory Shop
2 Aston Road, off Cambridge Road MK42 0JM
(01234) 217788

Curtain and upholstery fabric by the metre. Curtain-making. New showroom for range of high quality upholstered furniture direct from own workshops. Protective table felt; lengths of PVC.

'Large selection of ends of ranges and slight seconds.'

....

Off the A5134 (Cambridge Road) south-east of Bedford centre.

From town centre: head south over river, go straight at traffic lights, take second exit at next roundabout (London Road). At second roundabout fork left, go straight at third roundabout; take second left, Aston Road.

From Luton on A6: go right at roundabout for Elstow (A5134). At next roundabout go straight (Mile Road). At next roundabout take second exit (Harrowden Road), go straight over next roundabout into Cambridge Road. Take second left, Aston Road.

From A1, Sandy exit: take A603 for Bedford. After 5 miles go left at roundabout on to A5134 for Kempston. Take second right, Aston Road. Boynett 100 yds on left.

Open: Mon–Fri 9–5.30. Phone to check Saturdays.
Closed: Bank Holidays; Christmas–New Year.
Cards: Access, Eurocard, Mastercard, Visa.
Cars: On forecourt and street.
Toilets: Ask if desperate.
Wheelchairs: One small step to shop.
Teas: In local pub.
Groups: Groups welcome but must phone first.
Transport: Bus nos. 181, 182 to Hitchin; 176 to Biggleswade; 177 to Sandy.

11 Borehamwood Herts
Rubert of London
Unit 7, Stirling Industrial Centre, Stirling Way WD6 2BS
(0181) 207 2620

Vast range of quality ladies' fashions at least 20–40% off retail prices. Coats and jackets in wool and cashmere, knitwear, suits, skirts and blouses, raincoats. Complete summer wardrobe. No seconds.

'Offer a friendly personal service to our customers. Sundays very busy, so advise first visit on a weekday. Clearance sales in January and July/August.'

Open: Mon–Fri 10–4; Sun 10–2.
Closed: Saturday; most Bank Holidays, but phone to enquire; Christmas–New Year period – please phone for dates.
Cards: Access, Delta, Switch, Visa.
Cars: Outside shop or in nearby car-park.
Toilets: Yes.
Wheelchairs: Main showroom upstairs but items gladly brought down.
Changing rooms: Yes.
Teas: TJ's at Stirling Corner; also in Borehamwood.
Groups: Shopping groups always welcome: phone first.
Transport: Edgware tube station then taxi. Can provide transport if you phone first (weekdays only).
Mail order: No.

....

A few yards off the A1.
   Going north or south on A1: at Stirling Corner (roundabout, with Shell garage and 'TJ' restaurant, where the A411 crosses the A1) take small slip road in front of Curry's into industrial estate.*
   From M25 exit 23: take the A1 south for 3 miles and at first roundabout (Stirling Corner, with Shell garage on near left and 'TJ' restaurant on far left corner) take small slip road in front of Curry's into industrial estate.*
   *Pass BonusPrint on the left, then Stirling Industrial Centre on left and immediately go left into alley. Rubert is 50 yds on left.

12 Brighton E Sussex
Merchants Quay
Brighton Marina Village BN2 5UE
(01273) 693636   Fax (01273) 675082

Over 30 brand names for clothing, shoes, bedding, toiletries, cosmetics, ceramics, housewares, lighting, crystal & luggage.

'The relaxed atmosphere of a marina is combined with discount retail shopping in a variety of shops round the quayside. Facilities include a totally refurbished Asda supermarket & an 8-screen cinema. Many products at heavily discounted prices.'

See display advertisement inside front cover.

Open: Seven days a week. Shop times may vary but open 10–5 at least.
Closed: Christmas and Boxing Days.
Cards: Yes.
Cars: Multi-storey car-park.
Toilets: Yes.
Wheelchairs: Easy access within the complex.
Changing rooms: Yes, in clothing shops.
Teas: Several cafés, pubs and restaurants.
Groups: Shopping groups very welcome.
Transport: Local buses.

....

Brighton Marina is on the east side of town, below the high chalk cliffs.
   From Brighton town centre: go east along the cliff road (Marine Parade), following signs to the Marina.
   From Newhaven via Marine Drive: go left at sign to 'Brighton Marina Village' and follow signs down to the quay.

13 Brighton E Sussex

Kemptown Terracotta
Unit 8, 5 Arundel Road BN2 5TF
(01273) 676603

Terracotta pots (up to 20" high), urns, 'chimney pots', tubs – some with green glazed rims – and saucers. Unusual ridge tiles with large flying dragons. Guaranteed frost-proof.
'Perfects and seconds at reduced prices – price depends on extent of flaw but often half price. Small personal business so please phone first if you are making special journey.'

....

One and a half miles east of Brighton central pier.
From Brighton: go east on cliff road (Marine Parade) almost to marina. Pass large Georgian crescent set back from road with overgrown private park in front; look for railings in middle of road (start of dual carriageway): go left here into Arundel Road. *
From Newhaven via Marine Drive: go left to 'Brighton Marina & Kemptown'; after underpass go right to Kemptown; after gasometer go left at lights; go left at next crossing into Arundel Rd. *
*Park near The Bush pub. Beside pub go through archway to workshop at far end.

Open: Mon–Sat 9–6; *also April – end August* Sun 10–5; Bank Holidays. Best to check.
Closed: Christmas–New Year.
Cards: No.
Cars: In Arundel Road.
Toilets: Locally.
Wheelchairs: No access: pottery upstairs on first floor; showroom up further (sturdy!) ladder.
Teas: Pub and café nearby. Lots of places in Brighton.
Groups: Demonstrations gladly given to groups of up to 12 people; but must be arranged in advance.
Transport: Buses to Kemptown, nos. 1 and 38C. Volksrailway on seafront.
Mail order: Yes.
Catalogue: Yes. Free. Illustrated price list. No seconds.

A traditional Sussex craft

Trugs originated in Anglo-Saxon times, when they were produced by local farmers by hollowing out solid pieces of wood in the shape of their coracle boats. Known as 'trogs' ('boat-shaped') they were used as units of measure for bushels of grain and gallons of liquid.

They were updated in the 1820's when Thomas Smith of Herstmonceux modified the design to the now familiar basket shape. He exhibited his product at the Great Exhibition in 1851 where not only was he awarded a gold medal but Queen Victoria ordered several trugs for the royal household.

Smith received two gold awards in Edinburgh and London and then exhibited his trugs in Paris in 1855. He was awarded a silver medal with a certificate signed by Napoleon.

Updating the design for the twentieth century, Dudley and Laurence Hide of Hailsham developed the idea by making trugs from plywood – an idea taken further since then. Trugs sold today are based on this design.

Trugs were originally made for farm use but many people today find them invaluable in the garden. They are also used for decorative purposes in homes, restaurants and shops.

Thanks to Thomas Smith's Trug Shop in Herstmonceux.

The Factory Shop Guide for East Anglia & South-East England 15

14 Broxbourne Herts
Nazeing Glassworks Ltd.
New Nazeing Road EN10 6SV   *(01992) 464485*

Hand-made hand-cut lead crystal glasses, vases, glass ashtrays, candle-holders, decanters. Unusual items: wine carafes with own ice coolers; zodiac paperweights, apple-shaped apple sauce boats; melon, avocado, corn cob dishes. Range of items in black and coloured glass, especially Bristol Blue glass.

'Huge range of perfects and seconds, 50p–£70, usually 30% less than normal retail. Welcome special commissions, incl. engraving & ceramic decoration. Specialise in Ladies' Nights presents.'

See display advertisement inside back cover.

....

Just outside M25 (exit 25) between Cheshunt and Hoddesdon.
  From A10 (Great Cambridge Road): turn east for Broxbourne and get on to A1170 (NB If you are going north on A10, don't turn left for New River Trad. Est. but take next left). At traffic lights go east on to B194 for Nazeing/Lee Valley Park Lido. After Broxbourne station continue for 1/2 mile to small industrial estate on left; follow signs.
  From Nazeing on B194: go under pylons then over canal; after 1/4 mile follow clear signs into estate on right.

Open: Mon–Fri 9–4.30; Sat 9.30–3.
Closed: Bank Holidays; Christmas–New Year's Day.
Cards: Access, Visa.
Cars: Own car-park near shop.
Toilets: Yes.
Wheelchairs: One step to large shop.
Teas: Broxbourne.
Tours: Mon–Fri. Groups of 10–30 must book with manageress in advance. Adults 90p; children (must be over 5) and pensioners 60p; local school parties (within 5-mile radius) free. £2 refundable deposit for safety goggles.
Transport: Broxbourne station 1/2 mile. Broxbourne–Harlow buses stop outside.
Mail order: Yes.
Catalogue: Yes. Free: send large s.a.e. Selected range.

15 Bungay Suffolk
Nursey & Son Ltd. (Est. 1790)
Upper Olland Street NR35 1BO
(01986) 892821

Leather, suede and sheepskin coats, slippers, mittens, hats, handbags, gloves etc. for all the family. Leather gift items.

'Genuine factory shop with reasonable prices. Some seconds. Company supplies worldwide.'

....

15 miles south of Norwich, 15 miles west of Lowestoft, 6 miles west of Beccles.
  Coming into Bungay from the north side on A144: go through town, ie along Broad Street into Market Place. Continue on A144 towards Halesworth, along St Mary's Street, passing church on left. After 150 yds take right fork into Upper Olland Street for Flixton/Homersfield. Clearly marked shop 100 yds on right.

Open: Mon–Fri 10–1 and 2–5; Nov–Dec: also Sat 9–1 and 2–5 and late night Thur to 8.
Closed: Bank Holidays; probably last week July and first week August (please phone); Christmas–New Year.
Cards: Access, Visa.
Cars: Further down the road outside; small car-park opposite.
Toilets: In Bungay.
Wheelchairs: Access difficult, one step and rather narrow entrance.
Changing rooms: No.
Teas: In Bungay.
Groups: No factory tours; groups of shoppers welcome if they arrange in advance.
Transport: Eastern Counties bus no. 871.
Mail order: Yes.
Catalogue: Yes. Free. No seconds sent.

16 Burgess Hill W Sussex

Jaeger Factory Sale Shop
208 London Road RH15 9RD
(01444) 871123

Ladies' blouses, skirts, jackets and knitwear etc. Men's jackets, trousers, ties, socks and knitwear. Household goods including towels, linen etc.
'Perfect ends of lines etc.'

....

1/4 mile west of town centre, on the A273 (old main London–Brighton road).
 Coming south from A23 into town: keep straight on A273, follow signs to Brighton. Look for huge Do-It-All on right; turn left at second roundabout into Queen Elizabeth Avenue.*
 Coming north into town on A273: follow signs to town centre, turn right at first roundabout into Queen Elizabeth Avenue.*
 *Go immediately left into School Close, pass a block of flats, then go immediately left into gateway signposted Jaeger Factory Sale Shop.

Open: Mon 12.30–4.00; Tues–Fri 9.30–4.00; Sat 9.30–3.30.
Closed: Bank Holidays; Christmas and New Year.
Cards: Access, Amex, Diners, Switch, Visa.
Cars: Limited parking in car-park or on the road.
Toilets: In town.
Wheelchairs: Easy access, no steps.
Changing rooms: Yes.
Teas: In town.
Groups: Pre-booked shopping groups welcome.
Transport: 5 minutes' walk from town centre.
Mail order: No.

HOW TO FIND OUT where you can ...
- • visit plant nurseries, garden centres & gardens open to the public
- • buy your plants directly
- • talk to expert plant growers
- • gather new ideas & products from garden centres
- • gain inspiration from gardens open to the public.

The Road Atlas for Gardeners features ...
- • nurseries
- • gardens open to the public
- • garden centres
- • pick-your-own farms
- • 48 large-scale, full-colour road maps
- • clearly marked routes to all the places described
- • types of plants in which each nursery specialises
- • up-to-date opening days and hours
- • information for the disabled
- • and lots, lots more ...

The Road Atlas for Gardeners
for
Surrey, W. Middlesex, SW London & West Sussex

Our NEW easy-to-read, specially drawn road atlas is exactly what you need to plan outings to about 300 plant centres.

From good bookshops or by mail. (See order form, p. 94).

"I would like to say what a brilliant and informative collection your books are ... full of really worthwhile information ..." *Mrs TE, Peterborough*

The Factory Shop Guide for East Anglia & South-East England

17 Bury St Edmunds Suffolk
Carpet Bags
2000 St John's Street, IP33 1SP  *(01284) 700170*

Unique range of carpet, tapestry and fabric products: luggage, holdalls, gladstones, shoulder bags, totebags, handbags, pouches, purses, specs cases. Clothing includes men's and ladies' waistcoats and topcoats, ladies' jackets, boleros, trousers, hats, accessories, many in matching fabrics.

'Shop sales and mail order at less than usual retail prices. Further reductions on ends of lines and prototypes. Custom design and fabric selection by appointment only.'

....

In town centre.
   From A14 (the old A45): turn off for Bury St Edmunds Central A134. Go under railway, straight at two roundabouts and turn left at mini-roundabout by the gasometer.*
   From other directions and town centre: follow signs to Thetford (A134). Pass Burmah petrol and Honda garage on left then go right at the mini-roundabout by the gasometer.*
   *Then take first possible left: the shop is at the end on the near left corner (one-way street).

Open: Mon–Sat 9–6.
Closed: Christmas–New Year.
Cards: Access, Visa.
Cars: 1-hr parking by shop; all day parking 4 minutes' walk.
Toilets: In town.
Wheelchairs: Front of showroom is on ground floor, rear part down 2 wide steps.
Changing rooms: Yes.
Teas: Pubs, cafés, restaurants and fish & chips locally.
Groups: Small shopping groups welcome; no factory tours.
Transport: 3 minutes' walk from bus terminal (library); 5 minutes' from BR station.
Mail order: Yes.
Catalogue: Yes. £2, refundable against first order.

18 Bury St Edmunds Suffolk
The Factory Shop
Barton Business Centre, Barton Road IP32 7BO
(01284) 701578

Men's, ladies' and children's clothing, footwear, luggage, toiletries, hardware, household textiles, gifts, bedding, lighting, *Wrangler* and *Eastex* departments, and new fashion concessions department with famous brand names.

'Large stock of chainstore items, all at greatly reduced prices.'

....

On industrial estate on the east side of Bury St Edmunds.
   From A14 (the old A45T): exit at signs to Bury St Edmunds East and turn towards Moreton Hall Estate. Go straight at first roundabout (Sainsbury's on your right).*
   From town centre: follow signs to Ipswich (A14) via A1302 ring road. Go underneath A14 (old A45) and straight at first roundabout with Sainsbury's on right.*
   *Go left at second roundabout, then straight at the third and fourth roundabouts. Go downhill and turn left just before the railway bridge. Shop is in second building on right.

Open: Mon–Sat 9–5.30; Sun 11–5.
Closed: Bank Holidays; Christmas, Boxing and New Year's Days.
Cards: Access, Switch, Visa.
Cars: Own large car-park.
Toilets: In town.
Wheelchairs: Ramps available.
Changing rooms: Yes.
Teas: Cafés and pubs in town.
Groups: Glad to see shopping groups – phone call appreciated.
Transport: 20 minutes' walk from station; 15 minutes from town centre.
Mail order: No.

19 Butley Suffolk

Butley Pottery (NEW)
7 Mill Lane IP12 3PA
(01394) 450785

Individually hand-painted majolica pottery: teapots, mugs, bowls, jugs, terracotta pots, lamps. Dishwasher proof. Domestic ware and commemorative ware. Also work to commission.

'*Prices from £5–£150. Almost all items perfect with occasional seconds. Art and sculpture gallery on same site open Easter–Christmas. Short courses on creative subjects, eg painting, marquetry, writing etc – phone or write for details.*'

....

Butley is on the B1084 about 6 miles east of Woodbridge.
   Coming from Woodbridge: in Butley turn right off the B1084 at the signpost to pottery and village hall. The thatched complex is clearly signposted a few hundred yards on the left.

Open: 7 days a week 10.30–5 (*Easter–Christmas*) and Wed–Sun 10.30–5 (*February–Easter*).
Closed: Mon and Tues (*February–Easter*); whole of *January*.
Cards: Access, Visa.
Cars: In pottery yard.
Toilets: Yes, and for disabled.
Wheelchairs: Two steps to medium sized shop.
Teas: Thatched tea barn/restaurant open weekends (*Feb–Easter*) then 7 days a week (*Easter–Christmas*).
Groups: Potter can be viewed at work through the door.
Transport: Buses pass the end of the lane from Woodbridge.
Mail order: Yes.
Catalogue: Yes. Free.

---

20 Canterbury Kent

Essentially Hops
The Oast House, School Lane, Bekesbourne CT4 5ES
(01227) 830666

Wide variety of home grown dried flowers. Arrangements ready made and made to order. Dried hop bines (traditional Kentish garland 8ft long) for sale all year; fresh bines in September if ordered in advance. Mail order available.

....

2 miles east of Canterbury, near Howletts Zoo.
   From London on A2: after Canterbury exit, take slip road to Howletts Zoo/Bekesbourne.*
   From Canterbury: head for Dover/A2. Follow signs to Howletts Zoo/Bekesbourne.*
   From Dover via A2: take slip road to Bekesbourne/Bridge and Howletts Zoo. Keep following signs to Bridge village. Go through Bridge, then right to Bekesbourne. Go to mini-roundabout then to Howletts Zoo/Bekesbourne.*
   *In Bekesbourne, before railway bridge, go right into School Lane, following brown 'Hop Farm' signs – oast house 1/2 mile on right. (If you get to Howletts Zoo, you've gone too far!)

Open: Mon–Fri 12.30–5; Sat 9–5; Sun 12.30–4.30. Always phone to check. Bank Holidays.
Closed: For two weeks following Christmas Day.
Cards: Access, Visa.
Cars: Ample parking in field.
Toilets: Ask if desperate.
Wheelchairs: Access to ground floor.
Teas: Bring your own picnic; local pubs.
Groups: Tours at £1.75 per head (tea and biscuits can be provided). Please phone to book. Individuals free to look round.
Transport: British Rail from Canterbury East and Victoria.
Mail order: Yes.
Catalogue: Yes, free. Hops available – orders by September. Hope to bring in dried flowers & arrangements. Mixed dried flower boxes available.

The Factory Shop Guide for East Anglia & South-East England

21 Chichester W Sussex
Goodwood MetalCraft Ltd.
Terminus Road Industrial Estate
PO19 2UI
(01243) 784626

Wide range of Chichester stainless steel tableware (teapots, carving dishes etc), saucepans and stainless steel cookware; glass, china, porcelain, Russian dolls, wooden boxes, gifts. *'All at exceptional prices. Seconds and ends of ranges.'*

See display advertisement on p. 61

Open: Mon–Fri 10–3; Sat 10–1.
Closed: Bank Holidays; Christmas–New Year; one week late May and one week late August – please phone for dates.
Cards: Access, Visa.
Cars: In front of company, then walk 100 yds to rear of factory.
Toilets: Please ask.
Wheelchairs: Sizeable shop on 1st floor up metal staircase (no lift).
Teas: Tea, coffee available. Lots of places in Chichester.
Groups: No factory tours. Pre-booked shopping groups always welcome.
Transport: 1/2 mile from railway station and bus depot.
Mail order: No.

On the south side of Chichester.
From the north: follow Chichester ring road; turn off to 'The Witterings' and keep following signs. After crossing railway, pass The Richmond Arms on left; take next right (Terminus Road) to 'Industrial Estate'. Company 1/2 mile on left.*
From Portsmouth via A27: at first roundabout south-west of Chichester turn off for 'Terminus Ind. Estate'. Company on right.*
From Arundel on A27: stay on A27 (Chichester bypass), going round town; at 4th roundabout go right; go left for Terminus Ind. Estate. Company 1/2 mile on left.*
*Park at front; walk down drive on left to rear entrance.

22 Clacton-on-Sea Essex
Mascot Clothing
401 Old Road CO15 3RK
(01255) 432773

Ends of ranges and seconds of quality waxed cotton; breathable waterproof clothing for men, ladies and children. Tweed shooting jackets; quilted garments and hats, caps. Materials. *'Savings of up to 40%.'*

Open: Wed 12–4; Fri 12–6; first Sat in every month 10–1.
Closed: Bank Holidays; Christmas; New Year's Day.
Cards: Access, Visa.
Cars: Large car-park.
Toilets: Public toilets across the road.
Wheelchairs: Stone staircase to shop on 2nd floor.
Teas: Several tea shops and pubs in village.
Groups: Coach parties welcome by prior arrangement. Please phone.
Transport: Local bus 50 yds; BR station 10 minutes' walk.

North of town.
From Colchester on A133: turn left on to B1027 to Frinton and Walton at roundabout with fire station on far right. Go past Queen's Head Hotel then turn sharp right 20 yds after pedestrian lights: shop is first on right.
From town centre: follow signs to A133 Colchester. At crossing with Esso on far left, follow signs to B1369 Great Clacton. You are now in Old Road. Shop is on left in last building by T-junction.

23 Crayford Kent
David Evans and Co.
Bourne Road DA1 4BR
(01322) 559401

Silk fabric by the metre; wide range of articles in silk, woven or printed by the company. Ties, handkerchiefs, scarves, shawls. Ladies' and gentlemen's exclusive range of gifts, eg boxer shorts, handbags, purses, wallets.

'Lots of bargains in famous name seconds. All at mill shop prices. Ring for Christmas late nights and special sales, mentioning this book.'

....

From M25 exit 2: take A2 for London. Turn off at Black Prince Interchange for Bexley/Bexleyheath; following brown tourist signs, take first exit at first roundabout and third exit at next roundabout. *
From London via A2: exit at Black Prince Interchange on to A223 (for Crayford, Bexley, Erith), take second exit at roundabout, following brown tourist signs. *
***Pass Hall Place on right; shortly after Jet petrol on right (and 50 yds before T-junction) go right into Bourne Industrial Park.**

Open: Mon–Fri 9.30–5; Sat 9.30–4.30.
Closed: Bank Holidays; please check for Christmas–N Year.
Cards: Access, Switch, Visa.
Cars: Own car-park.
Toilets: Yes.
Wheelchairs: No steps to large shop, coffee shop or craft centre.
Teas: Own Mulberry Tree Coffee Shop for home baked produce, light lunches, cream teas etc. (01322) 529198 for catering manageress.
Tours: Pre-booked guided tours Mon–Fri to see hand-screen printing and finishing, and museum. Including video tour lasts 1 1/4 hours. Adults £2, OAPs and students £1.50.
Transport: Trains to Crayford. Buses: London Transport no. 96; Greenline nos. 725, 726.

24 East Dereham Norfolk
The Factory Shop
South Green NR19 1PP
(01362) 691868

Wide selection of clothing and footwear for all the family. Good range of branded bedding, towels, toiletries and fancy goods. Also health products, shoes and pottery.

'Large stock of chainstore items, all at greatly reduced prices.'

....

About 15 minutes' walking distance from the town centre.
From the centre: follow the 'A47 bypass' sign along London Road. At the traffic lights with Texas DIY on the near right, turn right towards 'A1075 Watton' then right again to 'South Green Industrial Estate'. The shop is 150 yds on the right.

Open: Mon–Sat 9–5.
Closed: Bank Holidays (but phone to check).
Cards: Access, Delta, Switch, Visa.
Cars: Own car-park.
Toilets: In town centre.
Wheelchairs: Easy access, no steps, but not advisable on busy Saturdays.
Changing rooms: Yes.
Teas: In town centre.
Groups: Shopping groups welcome but prior phone call appreciated.
Transport: Bus no.794 to town centre, then 15 minutes' walk.
Mail order: No.

25 Eastbourne E Sussex
Napier
3 Courtlands Road BN22 8SV (01323) 644511
Quality end-of-line and limited edition designer fashion jewellery in classic and contemporary designs direct from USA manufacturers. Classic chains, necklaces, brooches, hundreds of earrings, rings, chokers, bracelets.

'Quality merchandise at bargain prices. Items (all perfects) up to 75% off usual retail price, from £2.50–£500. Sale after Christmas. Ask to join customer list.'
....

On north-east side of town.
   Going south on A22/from A27: at roundabout go left for Sea Front & Town Centre (East). Stay on A2021. Pass Travis Perkins on right.*
   From Brighton on A259: follow signs for Hastings (A259)/A2040. Pass Travis Perkins on right.*
   *At 2nd lights, go left (Waterworks Road).**
   From town: with station on left, follow 1-way system. Don't go right to ring road (for Samaritans) but keep straight on Ashford Rd. At T-junction with lights, go right; at next lights, go left (Waterworks Rd).**
   From Hastings on A259: stay on this road, pass fire station on left: after 50 yds go right (Waterworks Road).**
   **Pass Unigate on left, follow road round and go left (Courtlands Road). Shop is on left.

Open: Mon–Sat 10–6; Sun 10–4; some Bank Holidays – please phone to check.
Closed: Christmas, Boxing and New Year's Days.
Cards: Access, Visa.
Cars: Own car-park.
Toilets: In town.
Wheelchairs: Ramp.
Teas: Lots of cafés in town.
Groups: Shopping groups welcome; please book first with Janet Wake.
Transport: 10 minutes' walk from nearest bus stop.
Mail order: No.

26 Fakenham Norfolk
Gilchris Confectionery Ltd.
1–2 Oxborough Lane NR21 8AF
(01328) 862632

Wide range of high-quality confectionery made here – chocolates, marzipan, biscuits, seasonal novelties etc, depending on what is being made that week.

'All items rejects, eg slightly scuffed and occasional misshapes.'
....

Very close to the town centre, on the south side.
   From Market Place: walk along to post office then turn down White Horse Street. At end go left into Oxborough Lane.*
   From Norwich via A1067: turn left at Fakenham Town Centre sign into Norwich Road, continue towards town centre. Go left at junction (White Horse Street) then left again (Oxborough Lane).*
   Coming north from Dereham (B1146): go over bridge into Bridge Street, look for Limes Hotel on left and turn right opposite it. Continue along Cattle Market Street. As road bears left, take right turn (Oxborough Lane).*
   *Company well marked on right.

Open: Thur 7.30–3. Also on four Saturdays before Christmas and Easter.
Closed: Bank Holidays; Christmas–New Year.
Cards: No.
Cars: Own car-park and also at rear of site; paid parking at Budgens.
Toilets: In Fakenham.
Wheelchairs: No access (tiny sales area).
Teas: In town.
Groups: Tiny shop; not suitable for groups.
Transport: Any bus to Fakenham then 5 minutes' walk.
Mail order: No.

Finding your way there!

Preparing directions for finding the shops takes an inordinate amount of time. What might seem on the surface like a straightforward undertaking can become very complicated and very time-consuming, especially in city centres, in heavy traffic and when you simply cannot avoid the almost inevitable one-way system. How simple life was when you could go both *up* & *down* each street!

Recognizing that some shoppers prefer to navigate by maps, while other people find it much easier to follow verbal directions, we aim to give accurate details in the clearest way possible. Densely built urban areas present the greatest challenge to preparing directions so that anyone can track down each shop from any direction. We presume that the average reader has basic maps and a road atlas of the country.

We are constantly taken aback by the frequency with which roads, road numbers, roundabouts, road signs and one-way systems change and how often petrol stations alter brand. If you notice such changes, we will be very grateful if you let us know.

To our loyal readers!

We visit the shops in our books personally. Over the last 10 years, our quest for factory shops has involved driving over 300,000 miles and visiting at least 6,000 shops. The time, effort and money for this research are very considerable!

Four years ago a Cardiff company published a book using our information, which we had gleaned over years of intensive personal effort. We took them to the High Court. We obtained judgement against them, and an injunction ordering them to deliver all the infringing books up to us and to pay our costs.

Even more recently a mail order company, which advertises widely in the national press, published a guide to factory shops which included information on nearly 700 shops which also appear in our books. While not admitting that any copying took place, this company reached an out of court settlement with us, withdrew its publication and paid our costs.

We own the copyright in our books, in the layout and in the compilation of shops which are selected. This means that it is an infringement of our copyright for anyone else to use our list of factory shops in order to prepare his or her own list. We have invested many years in *The Factory Shop Guide* and we will not hesitate to defend our right against unfair imitators. If you come across anyone else who appears to be infringing our copyright, we will be grateful to hear from you. Sincere thanks.

The Factory Shop Guide for East Anglia & South-East England

27 Fareham Hants
Grandford Carpet Mills
Unit 11, Bridge Industries, Broadcut PO16 8ST
(01329) 289612

Carpets tufted here: 4-metre wide heavy duty domestic range in various qualities from 100% synthetic fibre to 80/20% wool/nylon. Specialise in 80/20% heather mixtures. Also rubber underlay and accessories.

'Small family business also offering dye-to-order service (minimum 50 sq yds). Seconds sometimes available. Prices from £7.95–£15.95, about half usual retail prices.'

See display advertisement opposite

Open: Mon–Fri 9–5; Sat 10–4. Some Bank Holidays, please phone to check.
Closed: Easter; Christmas–New Year period.
Cards: Access, Visa.
Cars: In own forecourt.
Toilets: Ask if you are desperate.
Wheelchairs: Easy access, ramp to shop.
Teas: In Fareham.
Groups: Free tours for groups of up to 12; please phone Mr Copplestone first.
Transport: None.

....

On north-eastern side of Fareham, about 1 mile from town centre.
   From M27 exit 11: go towards Fareham; follow signs to Fareham Industrial Park at two roundabouts. You come into Broadcut.*
   From town centre: go towards A32; at huge roundabout, go left before Roundabout pub; at next roundabout go right into Broadcut.*
   ***Unit 11 is one of the brown buildings 400 yds on right, near new Sainsbury store.**

28 Faversham Kent
Nova Garden Furniture
Graveney Road ME13 8UM   (01795) 535321

Luxurious couch swing hammocks, synthetic resin patio sets, reclining resin chairs; tubular folding frames, parasols, sunbeds, other accessories. All frames with wide selection of cushion designs. Large selection of cast aluminium & timber furniture.

'One of Britain's leading manufacturers of attractive luxury upholstered garden furniture. Seconds, discontinued lines; many items half-price or less.'

Open: *March–Sept only;* Mon, Wed, Fri 10.30–2; Sat 9.30–3; Bank Holidays except Good Friday.
Closed: *October–February;* Good Friday.
Cards: No.
Cars: Outside shop.
Toilets: In Faversham.
Wheelchairs: Wide double doors, huge shop, no steps.
Teas: In Faversham.
Groups: Welcome to shop, please phone first, mentioning this guide.
Transport: Faversham BR station then taxi.
Mail order: No.

....

East of Faversham, 2 minutes from M2 exit 7.
   From M2 exit 7 and A299 (Thanet Way, main Faversham–Whitstable road): take B2040 for Faversham. As you come into town go right for Graveney.*
   From Faversham town centre: with station on right, follow road round to left. At traffic lights go right (B2040 for Whitstable). Cross railway; take first left, for Graveney.*
   From Sittingbourne via A2: stay on A2 to Shell petrol on left – go left for Graveney. Go right for Graveney Ind. Est.*
   ***Pass Nova factory on left: shop 150 yds on left.**
   From east via A2: take first turn-off to Faversham; keep going towards Faversham – company is on right.

24   *The Factory Shop Guide for East Anglia & South-East England*

Hops and beers in Kent

As you drive through Kent, you will be very conscious of the many hop fields and oast houses where the hops were dried. If you are near Borough High Street, south of London Bridge, look out for interesting architecture relating to the hop trade. Hop traders have been located in this area since the late 1700s, and because of river transport from hop fields in Kent and Essex to the London docks, it was a major centre in the 1920s.

Hop factors, agents for the growers, took samples from the hop bales to their showrooms, mostly in Borough High Street. They were single storey buildings with glass roofs allowing good light where the hops were laid out for view by the brewers' merchants. Bargaining was intense. Hops are expensive and it is possible to make expensive mistakes!

The enormous bombing in this area during the second world war damaged most warehouses. After the war they were rebuilt in Kent and Herefordshire, rather than the centre of London, and most traders have moved to Paddock Wood. Of the two or three hundred family businesses involved in the hop trade, just one company stayed in Borough High Street.

With thanks to The Guild of Guide Lecturers for this information

For fresh or dried hops, visit Essentially Hops near Canterbury.

Widely associated with the cultivation of *hops*, the county of Kent does not always come to mind in relation to *beer*. However, Faversham is home to the oldest brewery in Britain! At the turn of the century, Kent boasted over 60 breweries but Shepherd Neame is the sole survivor of this once flourishing industry. This brewery has been making ales since 1698, and long before that time local monks used local high quality spring water to make their ale.

Two-hour guided tours of the brewery all year (not Friday, weekends or Bank Holidays) at 10.30, 2.30 & 7.30. Phone 01795-532206 beforehand. Up to 40 people in a group.

The Factory Shop Guide for East Anglia & South-East England

29 Fenstanton near St Ives Cambs

The Table Place
13–15 High Street PE18 9JY      (01480) 460321

Extensive selection of Regency reproduction furniture in mahogany, yew and walnut for the dining room, sitting room and bedroom. Also Tudor/Jacobean reproduction furniture in oak. Range of solid pine furniture. Desk chairs, desk lamps, chaises longues, pictures and mirrors etc.

'Showcase for a dedicated company of cabinet makers and French polishers from the heart of Rutland. The quality has to be seen and touched to be appreciated. Commissions undertaken for individual designs. Can also colour match to existing furniture. Some items which do not live up to the high standard sold as seconds. Also showroom at head office in Oakham.'

See display advertisement inside back cover

Open: Mon, Thur and Fri 10–5; Sat 10–4; Sun 11–4.
Closed: Tues and Wed; a few days over Christmas (please phone to check).
Cards: Access, Switch, Visa.
Cars: In High Street.
Toilets: Yes.
Wheelchairs: Easy access to ground floor, but unfortunately not to upstairs showroom.
Teas: Free coffee; or tea on request.
Transport: Many buses from Cambridge or Huntingdon and St Ives.
Mail order: No.

....

In middle of the village – well signed, near the post office.
From Huntingdon on A14 (old A604): turn off for Fenstanton. *
From Cambridge on A14 (old A604): turn off for Fenstanton. *
*Shop is in the middle of the village, near The George (on same side) and near the Crown & Pipes (across the road). Look out for signs for the Milk Depot.

30 Flimwell E Sussex

The Weald Smokery
Mount Farm, The Smokery, The Mount TN5 7QL
(01580) 879601

Foods traditionally smoked here over oak logs and chippings: salmon, trout, haddock, eel, gravad lax, mussels; chicken and duck breasts, venison, Toulouse sausages. Also British and Continental farmhouse cheeses, wines, gourmet foods.

'Smoked chicken breasts £3.95 for 2; smoked Scottish trout £4.10 per lb; smoked Scottish salmon sides £20 per 2 lb sides; smoked Scottish salmon sliced £6.75 per 1/2 lb; smoked duck breasts £5.75 per breast.'

Open: Mon–Sat 9–5.30; Sunday in summer; Bank Holidays.
Closed: Easter Day, Christmas and Boxing Days.
Cards: Access, Visa.
Cars: Own car-park.
Toilets: No.
Wheelchairs: No steps.
Teas: In Ticehurst.
Tours: By appointment.
Transport: Bus stop outside. From south: go to Etchingham BR station; from north: go to Stonegate or Wadhurst BR station.
Mail order: Yes.
Catalogue: Yes. Free. Everything despatched by 1st class post. Phone orders with credit card.

....

Just off A21, on A268 eastwards towards Hawkhurst.
Going east towards Hawkhurst: the smokery is on the left.
From Hawkhurst: take A268 west for Flimwell. Look for Sunnybank Garage then smokery is 200 yds on right at top of hill (after Bird Park on left).

31 Four Marks near Alton Hants

The Village Furniture Factory
Unit 4, Hazel Road GU34 5EV
(01420) 562111

NEW

Quality reproduction furniture, made here, in mahogany and yew: dining and bedroom furniture; TV and hi-fi cabinets; book cases; desks etc.

'Try us for lowest possible prices eg, mahogany dining tables £169; Regency chairs from £59. Delivery can be arranged.'

On A31 between Winchester and Alton.
   From Winchester: take A31 north-east to Four Marks; pass Total petrol on right, go over pedestrian lights and take next right. Turn right into car-park behind Hinson Hire: showroom is to the left of it, opposite Windmill Pub.
   From Alton: take A31 south-west. Pass petrol station on right and the Windmill pub on the right, and after 30 yds turn left into Hazel Road. Go right into car-park behind Hinson Hire: showroom is to the left of it.

Open: Mon and Wed–Sat 10–5 (Thur late night to 8); Sun and Bank Holidays 11–4.30.
Closed: Tuesday; Xmas Day.
Cards: Access, Visa.
Cars: Outside showroom.
Toilets: Yes.
Wheelchairs: One step to big ground floor showroom, but no access to upper showroom.
Teas: Little Chef about 1 mile direction Winchester.
Groups:
Transport: Mon–Sat: bus nos. 64, X64 (Southampton–Guildford). Sun and Bank Holidays: bus no. 453 (Farnborough–Winchester).
Mail order: No.
Catalogue: Yes. Free.

The Factory Shop Guide for East Anglia & South-East England

32 Godalming Surrey
Alan Paine Knitwear Ltd.
Scats Country Store, Brighton Road GU7 1NR
(01483) 419962

Luxury knitwear in natural fibres including cashmere, camelhair and lambswool (sweaters, cardigans, slipovers). Brushed cotton shirts and polo shirts.

'Most stock perfects at half price and always some seconds. Camelhair from £20; cashmere from £55; lambswool from £17. Genuine factory shop.'

....

In Scats Country Store complex on B2130 on eastern side of town. From A3100, main road through town: turn on to B2130 to Cranleigh at traffic lights. After 50 yds go left into the Scats Country Store yard. Shop is on left as you go into complex.

Open: Mon–Fri 9–5; Sat 8.30–4.30.
Closed: Bank Holidays; Christmas, Boxing and New Year's Days.
Cards: Access, Switch, Visa.
Cars: Outside shop.
Toilets: In town centre.
Wheelchairs: Easy access.
Changing rooms: Yes.
Teas: In Godalming.
Groups: Shopping groups welcome provided they phone first. No factory tours.
Transport: 10 minutes' walk from railway station

33 Godalming Surrey
Kent & Curwen Ltd.
21 Farncombe Street, Farncombe GU7 3AY
(01483) 426917

Top quality men's wear – suits, jackets, shirts, ties, trousers, knitwear and sportswear including cricket sweaters. Large selection of top quality golf wear, silk ties made to order for colleges, clubs etc.

'Many perfect items at full price. Ends of line, samples and seconds at reduced prices in this genuine factory shop.'

....

Farncombe is a village a short distance north-east of Godalming.
From Godalming: take A3100 north towards Guildford. Look for the conservatory company on left then The Three Lions pub on left. Turn left into Hare Road. *
Coming south from Guildford on A3100: pass Burmah petrol on right, then take third right (Hare Road) in front of The Three Lions. *
**Keep going uphill to the T-junction; turn left. Shop is on right, just before the level crossing.*

Open: Mon–Sat 10–5.
Closed: Bank Holidays; Christmas–New Year.
Cards: Access, Amex, Visa.
Cars: Far side of the railway.
Toilets: Across the railway.
Wheelchairs: One very small step to medium sized shop.
Changing rooms: Yes.
Teas: Local pubs in Godalming.
Groups: Shopping groups welcome but only by prior arrangement.
Transport: Next to Farncombe BR station (direct service from London, Waterloo).
Mail order: No.

34 Grays Essex
Choice Discount Stores Ltd.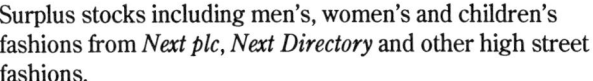
14–16 High Street RM17 6LV
(01375) 385780

Surplus stocks including men's, women's and children's fashions from *Next plc, Next Directory* and other high street fashions.

'Save up to 50% of normal Next first quality prices; seconds sold from 1/3 of normal retail price. Special sales Jan and Sept.'

....

In the pedestrianised High Street in the centre of town.
   From all directions aim for town centre. This gets you to the ring road around the centre. Park in any car-park and then walk. The shop is near the war memorial at the northern end of the pedestrian area, on the left as you go north.

Open: Mon–Sat 9–5.30.
Closed: Christmas and Boxing Days.
Cards: Access, Amex, Switch, Visa.
Cars: Town centre car-park.
Toilets: No.
Wheelchairs: No steps to large shop.
Changing rooms: No, but refund if returned in perfect condition within 28 days.
Teas: In town centre.
Groups: Shopping groups welcome! Book with store manager.
Transport: Grays BR station.
Mail order: No.

35 Guildford Surrey
Susan Walker Classics Ltd.
Astolat Garden Centre, Peasmarsh GU3 1NF
(01483) 577921

Top quality perfect Scottish knitwear in cotton, silk, lambswool, merino and cashmere (N Peal & Co. label) for men and women.

'Perfect quality at about a third of London prices – ladies' cashmere cardigans from £80 with occasional seconds.'

....

Peasmarsh is between Guildford and Godalming on A3100, about 2 miles south of Guildford.
   From Guildford centre: follow signs to Godalming. Astolat Garden Centre (with large name on roof!) is on left after 2 miles.
   From Guildford bypass (A3): take B3000 exit to Compton and Godalming, and continue to roundabout with A3100. Take first exit (left) and Astolat Garden Centre is on right after 400 yds. Shop is immediately inside main gates on right.

Open: Mon–Sat 9–5.
Closed: Please check Bank Holidays and Christmas–New Year opening.
Cards: Amex, Mastercard, Switch, Visa.
Cars: Plentiful free parking immediately outside.
Toilets: Yes.
Wheelchairs: One wide step into spacious shop.
Changing rooms: Yes.
Teas: Drinks and ice-creams at garden centre in summer.
Groups: Shopping groups welcome– please phone first.
Transport: Bus stop from Guildford/Godalming immediately outside Garden Centre.

The Factory Shop Guide for East Anglia & South-East England

36 Guildford Surrey
The Wilky Group Ltd.
Pembroke House, Mary Road GU1 4QB   (01483) 37131

Bathroom suites (basin, pedestal, lavatory pan, cistern, bath, taps, waste fitting) at trade prices for ends of lines. Also large standard stock at discount prices.

'Rock bottom prices. Perfect white and coloured bathroom suites from about £130. Lots of other bargains from this major distributor.'

Open: Mon–Fri 9–5.30; Sat 9–5.
Closed: Bank Holidays; Christmas–New Year.
Cards: Access, Visa.
Cars: Own yard.
Toilets: No.
Wheelchairs: One step to large shop.
Teas: In town.

....

From London on A3: exit for Guildford. At end of slip road go left; at next lights, go right; pass between Shell on left and Total on right. At next lights follow signs to Central Guildford (Renault garage on near left). Go under railway bridge, pass BP petrol on left, then take first possible right (just before pedestrian lights). *

From all other directions: go into town centre. Go around one-way system until you pass the court building on left with church opposite. At next roundabout go straight, then turn left after pedestrian lights (signposted to police station). *

*Follow this road around to the left: shop clearly marked 50 yds on right.

37 Hadleigh Essex
Choice Discount Stores Ltd.
14–20 Rectory Road
(01702) 555245

Surplus stock including men's, women's and children's fashions from *Next plc*, *Next Directory* and other high street fashions. *Next Interiors* and footwear.

'Save up to 50% off normal Next first quality prices; seconds from 1/3 of normal retail price. Special sales Jan and Sept.'

....

In town centre near Iceland.

From the west on A13: as you pass Safeway and Elf petrol on left, enter one-way system. *

From the east on A13: enter one way system with church on right. Take next right, following one way system, and pass Safeway and Elf petrol on left. *

*At next traffic lights go left (Bradford & Bingley on left): shop is 50 yds on right.

Open: Mon–Sat 9–5.30.
Closed: Christmas, Boxing and New Year's Days.
Cards: Access, Amex, Switch, Visa.
Cars: Car-park opposite shop.
Toilets: Public toilet facing store.
Wheelchairs: Easy access. No steps.
Changing rooms: No, but refund if returned in perfect condition within 28 days.
Teas: Tea shops in Hadleigh.
Groups: Shopping groups welcome! Book with store manager.
Transport: Hadleigh bus stop on A13; Rayleigh BR station.
Mail order: No.

38 Hailsham E Sussex

The Old Loom Mill
Mulbrooks Farm, Ersham Road BN27 2RI
(01323) 848007

Clothing fabrics (suitings, denims, woollens etc) and household fabrics (soft furnishings, curtaining, linings, sheeting). Wide range of fabric lengths, remnants. Comprehensive range of yarns for hand and machine knitters. Rug yarns.
'A dressmakers' and knitters' paradise. Fabrics about 50% below normal retail prices; yarns about 25% below. Annual sale starts 28 December.'

....

Six miles north of Eastbourne on B2104, just south of Hailsham.
   From north on A22: A22 becomes dual carriageway at roundabout where A627 and A271 join it. At next roundabout, go left for Diplocks Industrial Estate.*
   From south on A22: pass A295 right turn-off to Hailsham; go right at next roundabout for Diplocks Industrial Estate.*
   *Go through estate; at roundabout (Bricklayers Arms on far left corner) go straight on to B2104 for Hailsham. Shop is 1 1/4 miles on right, just after World on Water on right.

Open: Mon–Sat 9–5; Sun 10–4; Bank Holidays 10–4.
Closed: 24–27 Dec inclusive.
Cards: Access, Visa.
Cars: Own large car-park.
Toilets: Yes.
Wheelchairs: No steps.
Teas: Own tea room for home-made scones, cakes, light lunches. 10% discount for pre-booked groups.
Groups: Shop welcomes groups from clubs, guilds etc.
Transport: Trains to Polegate Station, then taxi. Bus nos. 21 & 268 from Eastbourne (infrequent).
Mail order: Yes.
Catalogue: No. Only regular lines supplied.

39 Havant Hants

Kenwood Ltd.
New Lane PO9 2NH
(01705) 476000

Small appliances including mixers, toasters, processors and irons. All graded, ie electrically and mechanically guaranteed for 12 months.
'Prices about 20% lower than shops. Brochures and prices on request: please contact Service Control, mentioning this book.'

....

Please note: this shop may be moving shortly. Please be sure to phone before setting out to check if shop is still open here, or to get new address.
   On the north side of Havant.
   From A27 (Chichester–Portsmouth road): go into Havant, right through town, keep straight. Go over large roundabout into Petersfield Road, pass The Curlew on right, go right into Crossland Drive for Havant Nth Ind. Est. At T-junction go right. Pass Kenwood gates on left; at next cross-road go left (Eastern Road). Go round cul-de-sac to Kenwood; shop on right.

Open: Mon–Thur 9–4; Fri and Sat 9–12 (closed Saturdays prior to Bank Holiday Mondays).
Closed: Bank Holidays; last week July/first week Aug; Christmas–New Year.
Cards: Access, Visa.
Cars: Outside shop.
Toilets: Yes.
Wheelchairs: 3 large steps.
Teas: In Havant.
Groups: Shopping groups welcome but essential to phone Service Control first.
Transport: By train or bus to Havant, then 10 minutes' walk.
Mail order: Yes.
Catalogue: Yes. Free. All items are seconds.

The Factory Shop Guide for East Anglia & South-East England

40 Hemel Hempstead Herts
Aquascutum
Cleveland Road, Maylands Wood Estate HP2 7EV
(01442) 248333

Wide selection of men's and women's suits, jackets, trousers, coats, knitwear. Men's shirts. Ladies' blouses, skirts, raincoats. Few scarves.

'Last season's stock, returned items, rejects, factory clearance lines. Occasional sales. Ask to go on mailing list.'

....

On the east side of town.
   From M1 exit 8: take A414 for Hemel Hempstead; go over first roundabout, right at second (to 'Industrial Area') into Maylands Avenue (A4147).*
   From town centre: take St Alban's Road (A414) for M1 exit 8. At large roundabout, go left into Maylands Avenue (A4147).*
   *Go straight at traffic lights; take first road to left (Cleveland Road). Shop on right, clearly signed.

Open: Mon–Fri 10–4. Please check times before visit.
Closed: Please check with company.
Cards: No.
Cars: Large car-park in front of shop.
Toilets: No.
Wheelchairs: One step to large shop.
Changing rooms: Yes.
Teas: In town.
Groups: Shopping groups should check with the shop beforehand.

---

41 Henfield W Sussex
Springs Smoked Salmon
Edburton BN5 9LN
(01273) 857338

Smoked fish including salmon, trout; also range of frozen shell fish, poultry, including smoked chicken. French fish soups, sauces etc.

'Smoked salmon from £6 lb sliced to £8.80 for best Scotch. Postal service available – please phone for details.'

....

4 miles south of Henfield, on Poynings and Fulking road. Well signposted, on main road in tiny hamlet.

Open: Mon–Fri 8.30–1.30 and 2–5; Sat 8–12.
Closed: Bank Holidays.
Cards: No.
Cars: Own large car-park.
Toilets: In emergency.
Wheelchairs: No steps to small shop.
Teas: Locally in Henfield.
Mail order: Yes. Please phone for details, mentioning this book.

42 Herne Bay — Kent

Peter Newman
Eddington Park, Thanet Way CT6 5TS
(01227) 741112

10,000+ shoes for all the family on display: Clarks, K, Rohde, Equity, Lotus. Shoes, boots, trainers and slippers.

'Branded shoes at factory prices. This company does not manufacture but these shoes are ends of ranges etc from their other retail shops. Prices considerably reduced.'

....

Large conspicuous shop on the A229 (Thanet Way) on the south side of Herne Bay.
   Shop is on the left, next to Texas, if you are going east towards Ramsgate.

Open: Mon–Sat 9–5.30.
Closed: Christmas and Boxing Days.
Cards: Access, Connect, Switch, Visa.
Cars: Car-park outside shop.
Toilets: Available on site.
Wheelchairs: No steps, huge shop.
Teas: Refreshment area with tea/coffee/soft drinks machines in store. Tea rooms in Herne Bay.
Groups: No factory tours. Shopping groups and coach parties welcome – prior phone call appreciated.
Transport: Herne Bay BR station. Go out of station, turn right, through alleyway to rear of factory shop.
Mail order: No.

43 Herstmonceux — E Sussex

Thomas Smith's Trug Shop (Herstmonceux)
BN27 4LI
(01323) 832137/833801

Three ranges of trugs plus some wooden fruits and gifts etc. Trugs in many sizes, made here, from sweet chestnut (rims and handles) with cricket bat willow; also in plywood. 'Walking stick' trugs, fireside log trugs, square and oblong trugs.

'Trugs at £15–£40. Personalised with pokerwork dates, initials to order etc. Most perfects but small range of seconds.'

....

In village centre, on A271, easy to see near turn-off to Stunts Green and Cowbeech.
   Coming west from Battle: go into village, round left bend, and company is 50 yds on left, with large sign 'Royal Sussex Trugs'.
   From Hailsham: as you come into village you will see the company on the right, just before phone box on left.

Open: Mon–Fri 8–5.30; Sat 9–5.
Closed: Bank Holidays; Christmas–New Year.
Cards: Access, Visa.
Cars: Car-park at rear of Woolpack pub.
Toilets: Across the road.
Wheelchairs: One step to small showroom. Wheelchairs can be assisted over step, door 30 inches wide.
Teas: Local pubs.
Groups: Gladly arrange an hour's tour for groups in working hours: please book with Robin Tuppen. Individuals welcome to walk round workshop. Small fee.
Transport: Any bus to village.
Mail order: Yes. Restrictions (no walking stick trugs sent).
Catalogue: Yes. Free. Only first quality trugs sold by mail order.

The Factory Shop Guide for East Anglia & South-East England

44 Hertford Herts
Lawthers Factory & Sample Shop
21 St Andrew's Street SG14 1HY
(01992) 504038

NEW

Large range of ladies' quality fashions, up to 50% off retail prices – jackets, coats (cashmere & wool); sweaters; skirts; dresses; blouses; rainwear and various one-off samples.

'Prices about 40–50% less than normal retail price. Chainstore items sold. Run a "house party circuit" with many top charities to raise funds on a commission basis – always looking for new customers for these parties, please phone for further details.'

In the centre of the old town near St Andrew's Church.
  Hertford has two railway stations, East and North. It is easiest to follow signs to very well signposted BR station Hertford North. If you arrive with the station on your left: go to the roundabout before railway bridge and backtrack on yourself. At mini-roundabout go straight, following signs to town centre. Pass Peugeot and Jet petrol on right, then the church on right, then The Three Tuns pub on left. The shop is another 100 yds on right.

Open: Mon–Wed, Fri and Sat 10–5; Thur 10–4.
Closed: Bank Holidays. Please phone for further details.
Cards: Access, Visa.
Cars: Public car-park behind shop.
Toilets: Public toilets close by.
Wheelchairs: One small step; not suitable for wheelchairs.
Changing rooms: Yes.
Teas: Scarborough's and various other cafés.
Groups: Shopping groups very welcome.
Transport: Hertford North BR station. Come out of station and turn right. Follow road into town and shop is on right.

45 Hickstead Village W Sussex
M & G Designer Fashions
Old London Road (A23) RH17 5RK
(01444) 881511

Wide range of upmarket designer label clothing for men and women at least 20%–70% less than normal retail prices. Sizes 10–26. Daywear, separates, cocktail wear, ballgowns, ladies' shoes.

'Some prices up to 50% less than retail, eg black pleated chiffon evening skirt reduced from £69.95 to £33.'

On A23 (old London–Brighton road), on north-bound side of dual carriageway south of Bolney.
  Going south on A23: shop is on far side of dual carriageway, so you must cross A23 and double back: take left slip-road for Hickstead Village/Twineham; cross A23 and go back north (following signs to Ricebridge) to warehouse 1/2 mile on left.
  Going north: take slip-road to Hickstead Village/Twineham. Go up to roundabout then straight ahead (following signs to Ricebridge) to warehouse 1/2 mile on left.

Open: Mon–Sat 10–5.
Closed: Please phone for Christmas and Bank Holiday closures.
Cards: Access, Amex, Switch, Visa.
Cars: Free large car-park outside warehouse.
Toilets: Yes.
Wheelchairs: One step; ramp available to sizeable shop.
Changing rooms: Yes.
Teas: Everyone offered free tea or coffee. Pub and café nearby.
Groups: Shopping groups welcome – please phone first. Coach parties can be accommodated.
Transport: None.
Mail order: No.

HAND-MADE FURNITURE DIRECT FROM THE FACTORY

At FURNITURE DIRECT every Settee, Chair, Stool or Sofabed we make will be individually tailored to suit your requirments. In addition to our comprehensive range of styles, choice of features, cushion fillings and sizes, we offer hundreds of quality woven fabrics, prints, linen unions and velvets. All this at a fraction of the price you would expect.

0% INTEREST FREE CREDIT
(written details on request)

FURNITURE DIRECT

46 High Wycombe Bucks

Furniture Direct
Riverside Business Centre, Victoria Street HP11 2LS
(01494) 462233

Quality upholstered furniture: sofas, upholstered chairs and sofa beds. Choose your own fabric from thousands available.
'All furniture made here. Also curtain-making service.'
See display advertisement above.

....

1 mile west of High Wycombe centre, just off West Wycombe Road (A40, High Wycombe–Oxford road).
  From High Wycombe: take A40; go over traffic lights with Europcar Rental on far left corner; after 100 yds go left into Victoria Street.*
  From Oxford via A40: as you reach High Wycombe, pass BP on right then The White Horse then Bird in Hand on right; take next right, Victoria Street.*
  *Riverside Business Centre clearly visible on left with large off-road car-park in front.

Open: Mon–Sat 9.30–5; Sun 10–4; Bank Holidays.
Closed: Christmas and Boxing Days.
Cards: Access, Visa.
Cars: Own car-park.
Toilets: Yes.
Wheelchairs: One tiny step, large showroom.
Teas: In High Wycombe.
Transport: Local buses go along the A40.
Mail order: No.

47 High Wycombe Bucks
GP & J Baker Ltd. & Parkertex Fabrics Ltd.

The Warehouse, Desborough Road HP11 2QE (01494) 471155

Wide range of curtain & upholstery fabrics: prints, damasks, jacquards, selected range of naturals; also wall-papers, borders.

'Britain's leading suppliers of fine furnishing fabrics and wallpapers. Large selection of near perfect and discontinued lines at substantially reduced prices.'

....

South of the town centre.

From M40 exit 4: at roundabout take 5th exit (to Cressex Industrial Estate). Go straight over mini roundabout; take next left by garage into Desborough Avenue. Go downhill past Kitchener Road on left; take second right (West End Road) before mini-roundabout. Go to far end; go right into car-park.

From London on A40: go right for town centre at triple roundabout; with huge College on left and fire station on right, go on to dual carriageway. Go left just after college for Desborough Road Shopping Area. At T-junction go left; keep straight to Bakers on left. Go left after company into side road (West End Road).

From Oxford on A40: at traffic lights (green Europcar on near right), go right for Wycombe Hospital. At double mini-roundabout, go left. Pass red-brick St John's Church on right; take next right.

Open: Sat 9–1.
Closed: Christmas, New Year and Easter weekend.
Cards: Access, Switch, Visa.
Cars: Yes.
Toilets: Yes.
Wheelchairs: Two steps into shop.
Teas: Cafés in town.
Groups: Not really suitable for shopping groups.
Transport: Local buses.
Mail order: No.

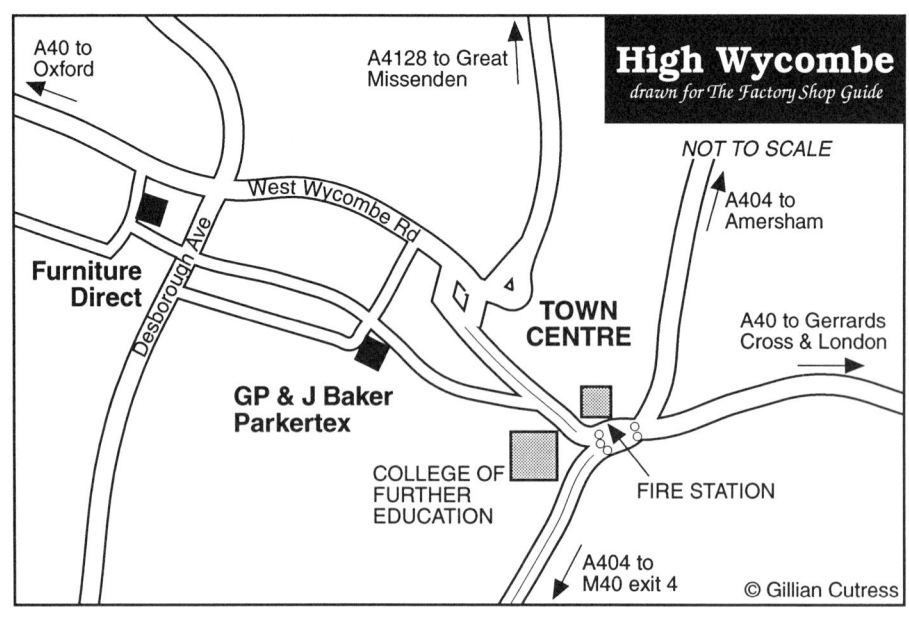

36 *The Factory Shop Guide for East Anglia & South-East England*

Ipswich Suffolk

The following two shops are in the same building, a few hundred yards north-east of city centre.
   From Colchester: follow signs to town centre. At roundabout with Civic Hall straight ahead, go left; go right at next roundabout on to A1156 eastbound.*
   From south and east: follow 'Through Traffic' signs; at roundabout with Civic Hall on right, go straight; at next roundabout go right on to A1156 (Crown Street).* Pass bus station on right, swimming pool on left. Pass Odeon on right; after 50 yds turn left into car-park.
   From Norwich/Stowmarket: go left on to A1156 for Ipswich; stay on it to Odeon on right. After 50 yds turn left into car-park.
Teas: Locals pubs and cafes.
Transport: Short walk from town centre and bus station.
Cars: One-hour parking 100 yds up road. Multistorey car-park nearby.

48 Broughton Shoe Warehouse
Tudor Place, off Woodbridge Road IP4 2DP
(01473) 233522

High quality Italian and Spanish men's and ladies' shoes.
'Save up to 50% on high street prices.'

Open: Mon–Sat 9–5; Sun 10–4.
Closed: Christmas and New Year's Days. Phone to check Bank Holidays.
Cards: Access, Switch, Visa.
Cars: Own car-park.
Toilets: No.
Wheelchairs: No steps.
Groups: Welcome.

49 Lambourne Clothing
Tudor Place, off Woodbridge Road IP4 2DR
(01473) 250404

Skirts, blouses, trousers, jackets; men's jackets, trousers, suits; waistcoats; knitwear and shirts; small range of T-shirts & knitwear, depending on season; tights. Some towels, bedding.
'Overmakes, seconds, ends of ranges, some samples of own label & well known high street labels. 10% discount for senior citizens.'

Open: Tues and Wed 10–4; Thur and Fri 12–4; Sat 10–1.
Closed: Bank Holiday Mons; last week July and first week August; Xmas; New Year's Day.
Cards: Access, Diners, Visa.
Toilets: Yes.
Wheelchairs: No steps.
Changing rooms: Yes.
Groups: Welcome to shop with prior phone call.

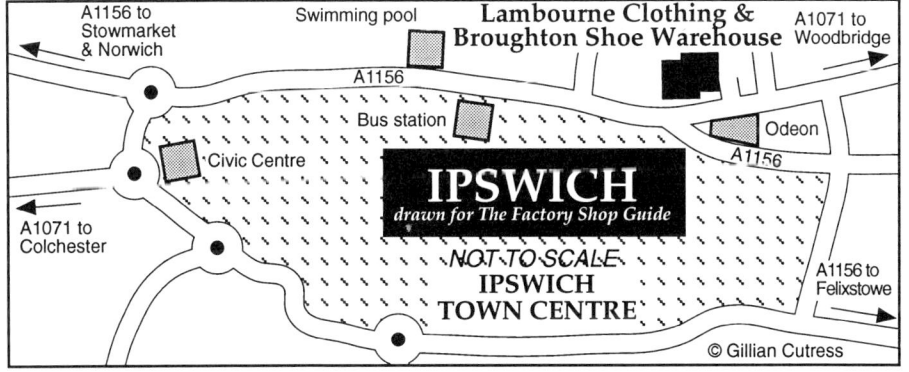

The Factory Shop Guide for East Anglia & South-East England

50 Isle of Wight : Alum Bay
Alum Bay Glass
PO39 OJB
(01983) 753473

Hand-made studio glass and jewellery. Vases, jugs, paperweights, animals, dishes.

....

As far west as you can drive on the island.
  From Freshwater Bay and Totland (A3055 or A3054): follow signs to Alum Bay and then brown sign to Alum Bay Glassworks. The factory is on the left just before car-park at the end of road.

Open: Seven days 9.30–5; Bank Holidays.
Closed: Christmas Day.
Cards: Access, Amex, Diners, JCB, Visa.
Cars: Nearby car-park (free in winter).
Toilets: Downhill from factory.
Wheelchairs: Easy access to large shop.
Teas: *Easter–end Nov.*: café across road.
Tours: *Easter–end Oct*: talks every half hour with demonstration. Adults 60p, OAP's 50p, children 40p. Parties by appointment only please. Self guided tours out of season. No glassmaking on Sat and Sun.
Transport: Southern Vectis bus nos. 1b, 1c, 17, 42.

51 Isle of Wight : Newport
Haseley Manor & Pottery
Arreton PO30 3AM
(01983) 865420

Pottery earthenware, mugs, cups, saucers, plates, dishes, vases, dinner sets, flower pots.
'Children's play area, picnic area. Historic house open during summer (admission charge to house).'

....

On the A3056 about halfway between Sandown and Newport.
  From Sandown: Haseley Manor is clearly signposted with brown tourist signs on the right.

Open: Seven days 10–6; Bank Holidays.
Closed: Christmas–New Year.
Cards: Access, Visa.
Cars: Outside shop.
Toilets: Yes.
Wheelchairs: Easy access to big shop.
Teas: Café in summer.
Tours: Free daily demonstrations.
Transport: Bus nos. 7, 7A, 48.

52 Isle of Wight : St Lawrence
Isle of Wight Glass
Old Park PO38 1XR
(01983) 853526

Designer glass, using gold and silver with glass. Vases, plates, urns, perfume bottles, paperweights.

From Shanklin on A3055: enter St Lawrence (signposted), pass the Rare Breed Park on left, then turn left immediately after the St Lawrence Inn. Follow brown signs to IOW Glass.
  From other end of island: enter St Lawrence and turn right just before St Lawrence Inn on right. Follow brown signs to IOW Glass.

Open: Mon–Fri 9–5; also in summer: Sat & Sun 10–5.
Closed: Christmas–New Year.
Cards: Access, Visa.
Cars: Own car-park.
Toilets: In hotel/café next door.
Wheelchairs: No steps to big shop.
Teas: In café next door.
Tours: Glassmaking Mon–Fri 9–4, ramps to viewing areas.

53 Isle of Wight : Yarmouth
Chessell Pottery (IOW) Ltd.
Chessell, Yarmouth PO41 OUF
(01983) 531248

Fine decorative, ornamental porcelain; vases, animals, fountains, dishes etc.

'Seconds available. Mail order service; please request a catalogue, mentioning this book. Collectors' Club with members' discounts.'

From Freshwater: take B3399 for Brighstone and Newport. After 3 1/2 miles fork left on to B3401 for Newport. Go right after 150 yds.*
  From Newport: take B3401 for Freshwater and the Needles. After 6 miles pass Calbourne Mill on right; after 1 mile go left.*
  *Follow brown signs to pottery.

Open: Mon–Sat 9–5.30; *April–Dec:* also Sun 10–5.
Closed: Christmas–New Year for 2 weeks.
Cards: Access, Diners, Visa.
Cars: Free car-park.
Toilets: Yes.
Wheelchairs: Full disabled facilities.
Teas: Yes.
Tours: Porcelain made and decorated Mon–Sat 9–5. Admission to studios: adults 40p, children (5–15) 20p.
Mail order: Yes.
Catalogue: Yes. Free. No seconds.

The Factory Shop Guide for East Anglia & South-East England

54 Kenninghall Norfolk

Suffolk Potteries
Lopham Road NR16 2DT
(01379) 687424

Wide range of terracotta storage jars, wine coolers, bread and flour crocks, plant and parsley pots, insect-repellent garden candles, Suffolk Smellies (pots impregnated with aromatic oil) etc.

'From £2–£65. Some seconds. All pots hand-made on potter's wheel in workshop. Viewing usually possible. Commissions undertaken.'

....

1 mile south of Kenninghall village centre, 2 miles north of South Lopham, 10 miles east of Thetford, 6 miles west of Diss.
  From South Lopham (A1066): take B1113 north for Kenninghall; Suffolk Potteries well signposted on left (2 miles).
  From Kenninghall market place (post office on left, White Horse on right): go straight for 1/4 mile then go south on to B1113 for N Lopham/Stowmarket; Suffolk Potteries well signposted on right (1 mile).

Open: Mon–Fri 9–5. Some weekends and Bank Holidays – phone to check.
Closed: Phone for Christmas.
Cards: Access, Visa.
Cars: Own car-park.
Toilets: Yes, incl. for disabled.
Wheelchairs: Easy access to small showroom.
Teas: Quidenham Tea Gardens about 2 miles north of shop. Swan House in Garboldisham about 4 miles south of shop.
Groups: Tours of pottery by arrangement – maximum 15 visitors. Contact Steve Harold. Groups welcome to shop if you phone first.
Transport: Sparse!
Mail order: Yes.
Catalogue: Yes. Free. Pots can be personalised and made to customers specification.

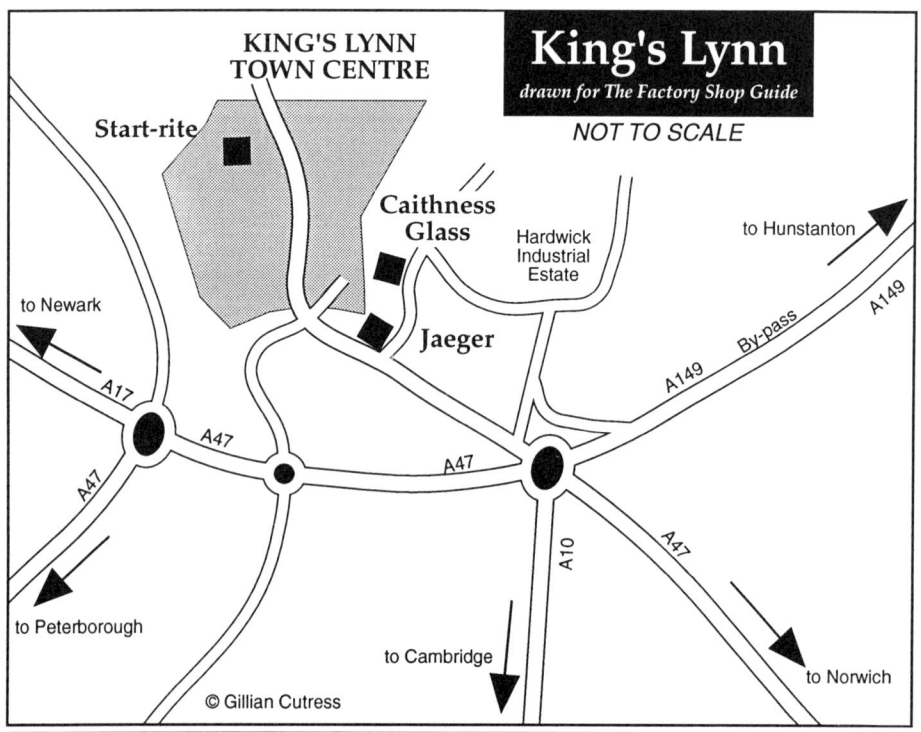

© Gillian Cutress

40   The Factory Shop Guide for East Anglia & South-East England

King's Lynn   Norfolk

The following two shops are close together, easy to find on southern outskirts of town.
   From town centre: go south towards A10 and Downham Market. Look for Campbell Soups on right; Jaeger is on the left, and Caithness Crystal in industrial estate on left.
   From the south on A10 or Norwich on A47: get on to King's Lynn southern bypass (A47/A149); exit for King's Lynn at large roundabout. *
   From west: continue on southern bypass to major roundabout where A10 joins. *
   From north: go left on to the southern bypass from wherever you hit the ring road. At major roundabout go to King's Lynn. *
   **Go along Hardwick Road. Take second right (Hansa Road). Jaeger is on the left. For Caithness Crystal, pass Comet on right and take second left (phone box on far corner). Shop on the left.*

Teas: Caithness Crystal restaurant for light lunches, homemade cakes. Shop hours. Plenty of places in town; Little Chef nearby.
Wheelchairs: No steps to either large shop.

55 Caithness Crystal

11 Paxman Road, Hardwick Industrial Estate   PE30 4NF
(01553) 765111

Large range of hand-made crystal glass. Coloured glass, eg wine glasses, tumblers, decanters, vases etc. Coloured paperweights.

'*Super bargains in well stocked shop. Personalised engraving. Factory seconds, discontinued lines. Christmas sale in Nov/Dec.*'

Open: Mon–Sat 9–5; *also Easter–Christmas* Sun 11–4.30.
Closed: Xmas and New Year.
Cards: Access, Amex, Visa.
Cars: Free for cars, coaches.
Toilets: Yes, incl for disabled.
Tours: Free self-conducted glassmaking demonstrations Mon–Fri 9.15–4.15; *also 27 May–7 Sept:* Sat and Sun 11–4. Need not book. See the glassmaker's skill at close quarters.
Mail order: Yes.
Catalogue: Yes. Free. Only factory seconds sold by mail order.

56 Jaeger

1 Hansa Road, Hardwick Industrial Estate PE30 4HY
(01553) 691111

Ladies' coats, dresses, blouses, skirts, knitwear. Men's suits, jackets, trousers, knitwear, shirts etc. Also household goods, hosiery, wool.

'*Quality merchandise at reduced prices*'

Open: Mon–Fri 10–4.30; Sat 9–3.30.
Closed: Please phone for holiday closures.
Cards: Access, Amex, Delta, Diners, Switch, Visa.
Cars: Outside shop.
Toilets: Nearby.
Changing rooms: Yes.
Groups: Shopping groups welcome with prior phone call.
Transport: Swaffham and Downham Market buses.
Mail order: No.

57 King's Lynn Norfolk
Start-rite Shoes
8 High Street PE30
(01553) 760786

Huge stock of footwear for children of all ages.
'Terrific bargain prices. Seconds and discontinued lines.'

....

High Street is a pedestrianised street in centre of town, parallel to (and west of) Tower Street. No. 8 is closest to the Saturday Market Place end of High Street.
   Park in any central car-park and walk to shop next but one to Debenhams.

Open: Mon–Sat 9–5.30.
Closed: Bank Holidays; Xmas, Boxing, New Year's Days.
Cards: No.
Cars: Town car-park between Tower Street and High Street.
Toilets: In town.
Wheelchairs: Large ground floor shop.
Teas: Lots of places in town.
Groups: Not suitable for groups.
Transport: Any transport to King's Lynn then walk.

58 Leighton Buzzard Beds
Gossard
Grovebury Road LU7 8SM
(01525) 851122

Gossard and Berlei bras, underwear and lingerie.
'Gossard and Berlei bras and lingerie at 1/3 to 2/3 of original retail price on perfect discontinued lines only. Seconds in all ranges. Please phone this genuine factory shop for occasional Saturday sales with special prices, mentioning this book.'

....

South of the town centre.
   From Leighton Buzzard: take A4146 south for Hemel Hempstead. Go right at mini-roundabout into Grovebury Road.*
   From Hemel Hempstead: go north on A4146 for Leighton Buzzard. Keep going straight to town outskirts. Go left by mini-roundabout into Grovebury Road.*
   ***Look for Gossard 500 yds on left.**

Open: Mon–Sat 9.30–5.30.
Closed: Bank Holidays; Christmas–New Year.
Cards: No.
Cars: Car-park in front of building.
Toilets: In town.
Wheelchairs: Ramp to shop.
Changing rooms: Yes.
Teas: In town; farmhouse along road.
Groups: No factory tours but pre-booked shopping groups welcome.
Transport: 10 minutes' walk from town centre.
Mail order: Yes.
Catalogue: No.

59 Little Horwood Bucks

Phoenix Carpets
Unit 17, Bacon House Farm MK17 0PS   (01908) 501019

Wool twist plain and heather tufted carpets in wide range of colours and widths in 80/20% wool/nylon and 50/50% wool/nylon or polypropylene mix. From 38 oz (general domestic weight) up to 50 oz (industrial use). Carpets can be made to exact colour requirements.

'Special service for making carpet in any shade and width (50cm–5m) you wish at no extra charge for minimum order of 20 sq yds (15x12 ft). Prices usually a few pounds below normal retail, eg 38 oz about £14. Organise complete fitting service.'

....

North of Little Horwood just off the A421.
   From M1 exit 13: follow A421 towards Buckingham. Go through Milton Keynes and Bletchley. Shortly after roundabout with sign to Mursley (left) and Whaddon (right) turn left (signposted to Little Horwood). After 400 yds take first left, between the first house and a pink bungalow, then follow signs.
   From Buckingham on A421: turn right towards Little Horwood at first sign. At T-junction turn left and after about 1/2 mile turn right immediately after the pink bungalow. Then follow signs.

Open: Mon–Sat 9–5.30.
Closed: Bank Holidays; Christmas Eve–New Year.
Cards: Eurocard, Mastercard, Visa.
Cars: Ample.
Toilets: Yes.
Wheelchairs: Easy access, no steps.
Teas: Can supply hot drinks on request.

Shopping in other parts of the country

If you find yourself in a new area of the country without the relevant Factory Shop Guide, don't despair! You should be able to get it in local bookshops, WH Smith, Waterstones, Dillons and James Thin in Scotland.

If you wish to have the latest details about our books, please send us an SAE. As we produce guides throughout the year, details about them quickly become out of date. Now that we have published so many books, we find that more and more people are returning forms which are two or even three years old – which means that there is a delay in sending the books. Which means in turn that there is a delay in getting down to the serious business of shopping!

If it takes too much effort to check which books are available, and their prices, it will be quickest if you send a blank cheque (ie payable to G. Cutress and signed but with the sum left blank) when you order. Write "*Limited to £16*" or whatever seems about right, clearly across it. We will fill in the exact sum & tell you how much it came to when we send the books.

If it is easier, **you can order your books over the phone or by post with your Visa or Access card.** We need the card number, its expiry date, and your name and address.

The Factory Shop Guide for East Anglia & South-East England

This self-regulating **Wringing and Starching Machine** is confessedly the best yet invented: its acknowledged Superiority, Cheapness and thorough Efficiency, together with the great saving in time, labour, trouble (and feminine patience withal) it effects, make it desirable for every family to possess.

We recently came across this marvellous advertisement (date about 1875) and as it, too, related to the Borough in South London (*see our reference to hop merchants in the same area*), decided to reproduce it here. This 'Little Giant' cost 17/6d (87 1/2p).

London

Many people assume that London abounds with factory shops. Yet apart from light engineering, very little manufacturing is carried out here. Production costs are generally higher than elsewhere in the UK and in the last thirty years many companies have moved to less expensive locations. Although small London clothing manufacturers continue to produce thousands of garments (especially in the East End), they tend to operate in small premises which are not open to the public. But the factory outlets which can be found in central and Greater London are well worth visiting and you will make real savings. We always keep our eyes and ears open, and if you have discovered other London factory shops, do please let us know.

The centre of London is always fascinating. If you are interested in fashion you will enjoy window shopping in the rag-trade district of W1. It is just north of Oxford Street, within the area bordered by Great Portland Street to the west, Cavendish Street to the north, Great Tichfield Street and Berners Street to the east, and Great Marlborough Street just south of Oxford Street. Many famous-name fashion houses are based here. The designs, colours, fabrics and knitwear are stunning, and seldom seen in such profusion in retail shops. If you are a keen dressmaker or knitter they will inspire you to greater heights. Although some showrooms are for wholesale and export buyers only, others have hand-written signs saying 'Public Welcome'. Look out for their summer and winter sales when bargains are offered by shops who, in the current economic climate, are glad of cash up front!

Skilled tailors ply their trade in New Cavendish and Margaret Street. We found one shop selling richly embroidered ladies' waistcoats, another with shoes at sale prices, and one selling men's casual shirts so vividly coloured that the Hawaiians should travel here to buy them. In between there are shops dealing in motor cyclists' outfits, textiles, fabrics, braids and trimmings, side-by-side with delicatessens and travel agents. Then walk across to the famous Carnaby Street, jammed with many small shops specialising in high-fashion items ranging from 'mod' fashion jewellery to leather western-style boots in a rainbow of colours. Berwick Street is home of the renowned fruit and vegetable street market. In this crowded street you will also find superb fabrics: sparkling sequinned cloth, velvet, satin, silk, brocade, shimmering stretch material, woollens, and novelty fabrics for toys and theatrical costumes. Berwick Street is a centre for the fashion jewellery trade with an amazing assortment of accessories – bracelets, earrings, necklaces, brooches, hair ornaments. Again, many shops are for wholesale or export trade only, but others welcome the public.

Information on London
Detailed information packs can be obtained from the London Tourist Board, 26 Grosvenor Gardens, London SW1 0DU (0171 730 3450) who also offer, on different numbers, a wide selection of recorded messages on *Places to Visit, Shoppping in London* etc. Their *Hotel Bookings Hotline* is (0171) 824 8844. Other central London Tourist Information Centres can be found at the British Travel Centre, 12 Regent Street (south of Piccadilly Circus) and Victoria Station Forecourt, both of which have an excellent range of guidebooks.

The Factory Shop Guide for East Anglia & South-East England

Another part of London where you can shop is the East End, the Whitechapel, Bethnal Green, Hackney area. There are masses of small shops although they cannot be called factory shops. Many describe themselves as 'Cash & Carry', others welcome retail shoppers as well as wholesale traders. Opening hours vary: most close on Saturdays, having their busiest period on Sunday morning when you can also visit Petticoat Lane market. But examine items carefully before you part with cash.

Here you will find oriental fabrics, and in Kingsland Road look for luggage shops and importers of foreign shoes (but mainly selling to the trade). Leather goods are sold to the public in Brick Lane. Towards Hackney is the furniture area where many small companies are delighted to serve the public. In Hackney Road you can find shops selling specialised products such as amazing ranges of balustrades, stair spindles, ornate radiator covers and lamp posts – items difficult to find elsewhere.

Designer clothes in the centre of London

Increasing prominence is currently being given to 'designer sale shops' in the press, and, in response to requests by our readers, we have recently spent several days walking round town to see what is happening.

Various shops in London offer reduced price designer labels; these may belong to a specific designer or brand name, such as the Paul Smith Sale Shop (0171 493 1287) in Avery Row, Joseph Sale Shop (0171 730 7562) in King's Road, Helen Storey shop (0171 437 0733) in Newburgh Street, Whistles Sale Shop in St Christopher Place, and Browns 'Labels for Less' (0171 409 7142) in South Molton Street. Shops are also being set up by people with special access to a particular brand, often Italian. You might visit the Designers Sale Studio (0171 351 4171) in King's Road, V IV M (0171 731 5567) in Fulham and other shops off Oxford Street, especially around St Christopher Place. Warehouse style shops (eg The Brand Centre in Enfield, 0181 805 8080) and discount clubs sell 'names' at reduced prices too.

Also, we were surprised to note how many second hand dress agencies have appeared, especially in well-heeled areas like Knightsbridge (as in Cheval Place) where you can indeed buy designer clothes at much reduced prices.

But 'factory shop' and 'designer shop' have become cult expressions, and are sometimes misused. We are in the privileged position of visiting thousands of shops all around the country, and feel justified in asking you to note the existence of certain down-market shops with poorly made (but expensive!) clothes, who claim to sell discounted designer outfits.

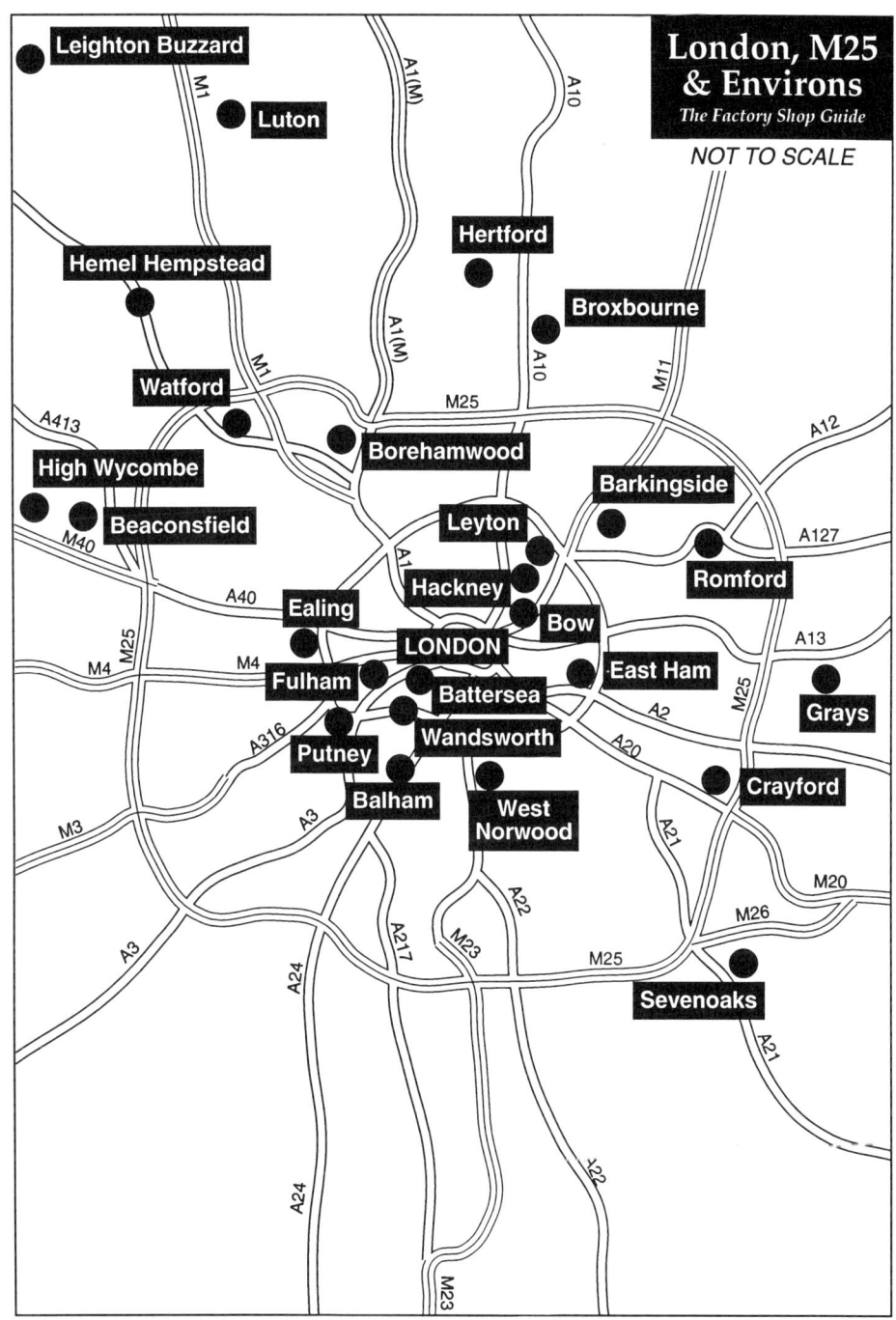

The Factory Shop Guide for East Anglia & South-East England 47

Markets in the Capital

Most capital cities have a huge variety of street markets and London is no exception. From antiques to modern hand-made crafts, jewellery to second-hand bikes, antiquarian books to designer boots, fruit and veg to an enormous selection of plants. There is something for everyone!

Many traditional street markets are still in the great outdoors, so dress accordingly! Whatever the weather, it is important to arrive early to pick up the best bargains. Bartering is generally expected, even encouraged, particularly when paying cash.

Some of the more famous open-air markets include:

Bermondsey Market (also known as **New Caledonian Market**), SE1. Open 4.30 am–12 noon on Fridays, so set the alarm clock! Here you find an extensive range of good jewellery, fine glass and china, silver, brass, maps and prints.

Farringdon Road Market, EC1. (Farringdon tube.) Daily. Allegedly a descendant of the 15th century Old Fleet Market. Old bound periodicals and lots of second-hand books for sale.

Portobello Road, W11. (Notting Hill Gate tube.) One of the longest street markets in Britain. During the week, mainly fruit and vegetables are found, but on Saturday (8–5) an enormous variety of traders descend on the street. Coins, jewellery, antique silver frames and art deco lamps, framed cigarette cards, African and Caribbean crafts, fabrics, clothing and lace abound. Dates back to the 19th century when it was a lively market for gypsies selling horses and herbs.

Columbia Road Market, E2. (Bethnal Green tube.) Sun (inc. Easter Day) 7–2. The market for plants. Gardeners and would-be gardeners will be sorely tempted by the huge variety of plants, bulbs, evergreens, annuals, shrubs and climbers. A hat shop has recently opened.

Petticoat Lane. E1. (Liverpool Street or Aldgate East stations.) Sun, 9–2. This huge market is actually centred around Middlesex Street, E1, and spreads out into neighbouring streets. Many bargains to be found here, particularly clothes, shoes, handbags and jewellery. A lot of junk is also sold, so choose carefully. However, it is fun simply to watch the colourful characters tout their wares!

Roman Road, E1. (Bethnal Green tube.) Mon–Fri 10–2; Sat 9–5. Saturday is the best day for this haven for fashion victims. Knock-off designer clothes, sold alongside fruit and veg.

Camden Lock. (Camden Town or Chalk Farm stations.) Sat and Sun 9–6. A bohemian mix of crafts, bric-a-brac, health foods and jewellery, plus much more.

Thanks to the London Tourist Board for these details.

Leather Lane, EC1. (Chancery Lane tube.) Mon–Fri 10–2.30 (except Bank Holidays). Wonderful bulbs and plants in season, clothes, shoes, household goods, fruit and veg.

For the colder, wetter days, there are numerous covered markets, the best-known of which include :

Greenwich Market, SE1. Sat (all year) and Sun from Easter to September 9–5. Housed under a Nash-style arched roof built in 1831, and a great place for Christmas shopping. Handknits, silk cushions and ties, clocks, earrings and ceramics are just some of the goods here.

Leadenhall Market, Gracechurch Street, EC3. (Monument tube.) Mon–Fri 9–5. This is situated right in the heart of the city. Although technically a street market, a wooden arched roof protects the stalls from the elements. A huge variety of poultry, game and seafood are the specialities here. The market was built in 1881 and the historic feel is emphasised by the period decor and olde worlde culinary delights. Numerous pubs and restaurants refresh weary shoppers!

Apple Market and **Jubilee Market Hall**, Old Covent Garden, WC2. (Covent Garden tube.) Tues–Sat 10–7, Mon 7–7; Sun 9–7. These markets are situated on the historic market site of Covent Garden. They sell a huge variety of crafts, including hand-painted silk cushions, toy clocks, ceramics and handknits. On Monday and the first Sunday of every month, antiques are the speciality.

Alfies Market, 13–25 Church Street, NW8. (Edgware Road tube.) Tues–Sat 10–6. Housed in a former department store, this market specialises in antiques.

Camden Passage, N1. (Angel tube.) Wed 6.45–4; Thur 7–4; Sat 8–5. Another market specialising in antiques. On Thursday, prints and drawings are also sold.

For a totally different experience, try one of the famous wholesale markets. These start very early in the morning and can be found at :

Smithfield, EC1. (Farringdon tube.) For meat, poultry, game (and excellent local pubs open for breakfast!).

Billingsgate, E14, for fish.

New Covent Garden, SW8, and Borough, SE1, for fruit, vegetables and flowers.

This is not an exhaustive list of markets to be found around London, but should give plenty of food for thought!

The Factory Shop Guide for East Anglia & South-East England   *49*

60 London : Balham
Indian Ocean Trading Company
28 Ravenswood Road SW12 9PJ
(0181) 675 4808   Fax (0181) 675 4652

NEW

Top quality classic teak-framed garden furniture: benches, chairs, tables, deckchairs, folding chairs, tree seats, hammocks, planters, sunshades, cushions, croquet sets.

'This manufacturer offers widest selection of teak garden furniture in Britain (all wood from managed forests). Prices below those for equivalent quality in stores/garden centres (refund difference if you find same quality for lower price!). Free 'see it in your own garden' service. Delivery in UK £15.'

....

In a residential road off (east of) Balham High Road (A24).

Coming south (ie, from London direction) along Balham High Road: pass Total petrol on right, go over pedestrian lights then take first left (opposite Salvation Army) into Ravenswood Road.*

Coming north (ie, from Tooting Bec/Balham) along Balham High Road: go over pedestrian lights (Duke of Devonshire pub on right); take next right (opposite Salvation Army) into Ravenswood Rd.*

*Clearly marked company is 50 yds on right.

From Cavendish Road: at the corner with Magnet, turn into Ravenswood Road. Clearly marked company is 100 yds on left.

Open: *Mar–Sept:* Mon–Fri 9–6.30; Sat 10–6; Sun 10.30–4.30; *Oct–Feb:* Mon–Fri 9–5.45; Sat and Sun by appointment.
Closed: Christmas, Boxing and New Year's Days.
Cards: Access, Amex, Delta, Diners, Switch, Visa.
Cars: In street.
Toilets: Yes.
Wheelchairs: No steps to large showroom.
Teas: Local pubs and restaurants.
Groups: No factory tours.
Transport: Between Clapham South and Balham tube stations. Lots of buses along Balham High Street.
Mail order: Yes.
Catalogue: Yes. Write or phone for free catalogue.

61 London : Battersea
Price's Patent Candle Co. Ltd.
100 York Road SW11 3RV   *(0181) 801 2030*

Large selection of candles, holders and accessories suitable for every occasion: Christmas candles, novelties, dinner candles, church, decorative, catering, party, floating, scented, patterned and garden. Brassware, silverware, wrought iron, coloured glassware, napkins, flower rings etc.

'Bargains always available – discontinued lines, damaged stock and lots more! Please phone about sales and to check opening hours (often seasonal) before arriving. Huge discounts. New shop opening at Bicester Village, phone London shop for details.'

....

Immediately south of the Thames, between Wandsworth and Battersea bridges.

Going east along York Road from Wandsworth Bridge: pass Texas Homecare on left, go over traffic lights (shop was formerly on left in York Place, but this is now the trade counter) and shop is 50 yds further along the main road on the left.

Going west along York Road towards Wandsworth: go over traffic lights (Latchmere theatre pub on far left); go under railway, straight at lights. Immediately after Dovercourt/Audi garage on the right, clearly marked shop is on the right.

Open: Mon–Fri 9.30–5.30; Sat 10–5.30; (Sun 10–5.30 during summer and Christmas sales).
Closed: Bank Holidays; Xmas Eve (pm)–New Year.
Cards: Access, Connect, Switch, Visa.
Cars: Own parking spaces off road.
Toilets: No.
Wheelchairs: Seven shallow steps to medium sized shop.
Teas: Wide selection of cafés, restaurants and pubs in Battersea Park Road.
Groups: Factory tours for up to 12 people. Please phone Lynette Coetzee.
Transport: Local buses.

62 London : Bow
Nicole Farhi/French Connection
75–83 Fairfield Road E3 3QP
(0181) 981 3931

Nicole Farhi jackets, skirts, trousers, blouses, knitwear; French Connection knitwear, blouses, skirts etc.
'Previous season's stock plus samples and some seconds.'

....

In Bow, just north of the A11 / A12 (Bow Road).
  From London going east along Bow Road: pass Bow Road tube station on right then go left at traffic lights immediately after white concrete old Poplar Town Hall (and in front of NatWest bank) into Fairfield Road. Go under railway bridge: shop on left.
  Going west towards London on A12: from large roundabout/overpass on A12 where Blackwall Tunnel road goes south, go north on to A102 (ie do NOT take overpass); take left slip road (A1030) for Old Ford; at top of slip road go left into Tredegar Road; after 150 yds go left into Fairfield Road. Company on right, 50 yds before railway bridge.

Open: Tues and Wed 10–3; Thur 11–6.30; Fri 10–5.30; Sat 10–3.
Closed: Mondays; Bank Holidays; Christmas–N Year.
Cards: Access, Visa.
Cars: In street outside.
Toilets: No.
Wheelchairs: No step, small shop.
Changing rooms: Yes.
Teas: Local pubs and cafés.
Groups: Shopping groups welcome if you phone first.
Transport: Local buses. Bow Road tube station. Bow Church station on Docklands Light Railway.
Mail order: No.

63 London : Bromley-by-Bow
The Furniture Mill
32–34 St Leonards Street E3 3BS
(0181) 983 1654

Reproduction mahogany and yew bookcases, pedestal desks, bureaux, captain chairs, dining tables and chairs, TV, video and hi-fi cabinets. Chests and occasional tables.
'Furniture made on-site. Mainly firsts and occasional seconds. About half normal store prices.'

....

Near junction of A11 and Blackwall Tunnel approach road (A102).
  From central London on A11: at the huge junction with the flyover, turn off towards Blackwall Tunnel (ie, do NOT go over overpass) but then go around roundabout until you head back to London again. *
  From the east on A11: cross the A102 via the flyover. *
  From the north or south on A102: turn towards London on A11. *
  *Take 1st left into Bromley High Street (one-way). Pass Moulders Arms on right and take second right. Company is 300 yds on right.

Open: Mon–Thur 10.30–3; Sat 9.30–1.
Closed: Fri; Bank Holidays.
Cards: Access, Visa.
Cars: In yard.
Toilets: No.
Wheelchairs: One step to medium-sized shop.
Teas: Pie in the Sky Café 100 yds.
Groups: Small groups welcome for factory tours. Please book through Mr Major.
Transport: Bromley-by-Bow tube station. Bow Church station on Docklands Light Railway then short walk.
Mail order: No.

64 London : Ealing
Corcoran & May
11 Ealing Green, High Street W5 5DA
(0181) 567 4324

Fabrics for curtains and furnishing. Top designers such as *Parkertex, GP & J Baker, Colefax & Fowler, Monkwell and Christian Fischbacher* all use Corcoran & May to dispose of seconds and overstocks. Thousands of metres available at any one time. Curtains and blinds made-to-measure.

'Many fabrics less than half recommended retail price. Average price £9.95.'

....

Near the Broadway Shopping Centre.
   From central London along Uxbridge Road (A4020): turn left directly after Marks & Spencer into the High Street. Shop is just before the mini-roundabout, on left-hand side.
   From M4 exit 2: at roundabout go north (right if you come from London) into South Ealing Road. After 1 mile this road becomes The Green: shop is on right-hand side.

Open: Mon–Sat 10–5.30.
Closed: Bank Holidays, Christmas–New Year.
Cards: Access, Visa.
Cars: Many public car-parks nearby.
Toilets: Yes.
Wheelchairs: No steps to medium sized shop.
Teas: Local coffee shops nearby.
Transport: Ealing Broadway BR station and tube. Bus no. 207.

---

65 London : East Ham
Paul Simon Furnishings (London)
Kempton Mews, Kempton Road   (0181) 472 2333

Soft furnishings. Huge range of curtain and upholstery fabrics, over 100,000 yds always in stock. Net curtains in all styles and sizes. Large selection of ready-made curtains incl. extra wide and extra long sizes. Ready-made blinds and custom-made blinds. Curtain rails, tapes and accessories.

'50 machinists on site who will make your curtains to measure. Free measuring service within 50-mile radius.'
5% discount at point of sale on production of this book.

....

Just off East Ham High Street North.
   From London on A124 (Barking Rd): cross High Street at lights (Barclays near right, town hall on far right corner); take first left.*
   From Barking on A124 (Barking Rd): turn right into Keppel Rd opposite East Ham town hall (20 yds past Millers Well pub).*
   From A13 (Newham Way): at junction with flyover, don't go over flyover! but turn north on to A117 (Beckton FC and dry ski slope clearly visible south of this junction). Continue to traffic lights at Barking Road (Barclays Bank on left, town hall on right): go right (you can't go straight). Then take first left.*
   ***Kempton Rd is 3rd left (mini roundabout). Shop 300 yds on left.**

Open: Mon–Sat 9–6; Sun 10–4; Bank Holidays 10–4.
Closed: Christmas and New Year's Days.
Cards: Access, Switch, Visa.
Cars: In own yard, free of charge.
Toilets: Yes.
Wheelchairs: Small ramp to huge shop.
Teas: In high street nearby.
Groups: Can see curtain manufacture by appointment Monday–Friday.
Transport: 5 minutes' walk from East Ham tube. Turn left from station and take sixth left.

66 London : Fulham
Roger Lascelles Clocks
29 Carnwath Road SW6 3HR
(0171) 731 0072

Highly distinctive award-winning range of traditionally inspired quartz clocks featuring dial designs taken from antique clocks of the last century. Available in all major departments and leading gift shops.

'Seconds and previous year's lines at half price; regular lines at competitive retail prices. "The ideal gift". Family business.'

....

Immediately north of Wandsworth Bridge.
   From Chelsea/Fulham/Central London: go along King's Road until it becomes New King's Road. Go left down Wandsworth Bridge Road. Carnwath Road is last right turn before bridge. *
   From south London: go over Wandsworth Bridge; take first left (Carnwath Road). *
   ***After 200 yds, pass Fulham Kitchen Centre on left; go in through gates. Company is at back right.**

Open: Mon–Fri 9–4.30.
Closed: Bank Holidays; Christmas Eve–New Year.
Cards: Access, Visa.
Cars: Off-street directly outside factory.
Toilets: Yes.
Wheelchairs: Easy access, no steps to small shop.
Teas: Lots of places in locality. Easy walk to excellent riverside pub.
Groups: Phone Mrs Winship about free tours. Max 15 adults. Flexible times.
Transport: District Line tube to Fulham Broadway, then 28 or 295 bus to Wandsworth Br.
Mail order: Yes.
Catalogue: Yes. Free. Mail order service to anywhere in the world – please mention this guide when asking for catalogue. No seconds by mail.

67 London : Hackney
Hanging Garments (Burberrys)
29–53 Chatham Place E9 6LR
(0181) 985 3344

Men's and women's raincoats, trenchcoats, knitwear, shirts, skirts; accessories including umbrellas, scarves, handbags. Golf shoes. Jams, teas, coffee, chocolates, sauces, vinegar. Room sprays, fragrant cushions, pot pourris.

'Overmakes, seconds and ends of ranges. Not available in other Burberry shops.'

....

Just east of Mare Street (A107), the main north–south road through Hackney.
   Going south along Mare Street: go under railway bridge, go left at traffic lights (Morning Lane) for Bow/Leyton. *
   Coming north on Mare Street: pass Hackney Central Library (stone building with classical columns on right corner site); go right at traffic lights for Bow/Leyton (B113). ***After 400 yds pass Duke of Wellington pub on right; immediately go right (Chatham Place). Go in Burberrys' main door 150 yds on right.**

Open: Mon–Fri 12–6; Sat 9–3.
Closed: Please check with company.
Cards: Access, Visa.
Cars: Local streets.
Toilets: No.
Wheelchairs: Huge shop on first floor up stone staircase.
Teas: Some pubs and cafés in Hackney.
Groups: Please contact shop.
Transport: Buses and trains to Mare Street.

68 London : Hackney

The Factory Shop (Sofa to Bed)
Unit 1, Bayford Street E8
(0181) 533 0915

Sofas, sofa beds, lounge suites and divan sets. Matching curtains.

'All pieces made to order (some display models available). Also re-upholstery and re-covering services.'

....

Coming south down Mare Street (A107) towards London: pass Cordwainer's College on left. Go over traffic lights and take first right, Bayford Street.*
  From London along Mare Street (A107): after Texaco on right and BP on left (before traffic lights at major junction with Wells Street) go left into Bayford Street (letter box on corner) opposite old cinema.*
  After 30 yds go right, then left into complex with six units.

Open: Mon–Fri 8–5.30; Sat 10–4.30; Sun 10–2.30. Bank Holidays.
Closed: Christmas and Boxing Days.
Cards: Access, Visa.
Cars: On forecourt.
Toilets: Yes.
Wheelchairs: One step to large shop.
Teas: Cup of tea gladly made for customers; cafés nearby.
Tours: Welcome to walk round workshop adjacent to showroom.
Transport: Bethnal Green station; bus nos. 26, 48, 55, 106, 236, 253, 277, D6.

69 London : Leyton

R P Ellen
46 Church Road E10 5JR   (0181) 539 6872

Top quality ladies' leather fashion shoes, boots and sandals; some matching handbags. Some Church's ladies' shoes, Doc Martens and a few men's shoes.

'Company is a leading wholesaler selling shoes from Britain, Italy, Spain and Portugal. Most items perfect, some seconds and quite a few samples in sizes 3 and 4 at very reasonable prices. From £5–£30, most about £20.'

....

Opposite Leyton Parish Church, just off one-way system in Leyton High Road. Shop is 3/4 mile south of Lea Bridge Road (A104) but take care – restricted turning off this road.
  Going along Lea Bridge Road east for Walthamstow: pass Lea Bridge station on left, go over traffic lights with public toilets on island (this is Church Road but no right turn!); pass Shell petrol on left, take next right, Vicarage Road.*
  Going south on Lea Bridge Rd to Hackney Marshes: go over Bakers Arms junction, pass exhaust centre on right, go left, Vicarage Rd.*
  At far end (opposite Jet petrol) go right; after 100 yds you are in one-way system. Keep clockwise, pass Wilmot Street on left, take next left. Shop 150 yds on left.

Open: Mon–Sat 10–4.
Closed: Bank Holidays; Christmas & New Year.
Cards: No.
Cars: Own yard in front of shop.
Toilets: At junction with Lea Bridge Road.
Wheelchairs: One step to medium sized shop.
Teas: Local pubs and cafés.
Groups: Pre-booked shopping groups welcome.
Transport: Local buses; 10 minutes' walk to Leyton tube station or Leyton Midland Rd.

London : Hatton Garden

The street called Hatton Garden *[nearest tube station: Chancery Lane]* offers a greater selection of jewellery than anywhere else in Britain. The range of jewellery (modern, second-hand and antique) and gemstones is quite overwhelming; if you are seeking a specific item, make sure you allow enough time in which to browse!

Just outside the walls of the City of London, it was an area where qualified and skilled craftsmen congregated when waves of immigrants arrived in this country from various European states.

As with other trades, goldsmiths and silversmiths had to undertake a 7-year apprenticeship within the City in order to join a City guild and practice their trade. By operating nearby, yet outside the jurisdiction of the guilds, they were able to ply their trade without undergoing further training.

Hugenot jewellers and watchmakers, persecuted in their own countries, arrived from France and the Netherlands at the end of both the sixteenth and seventeenth centuries; Italians (famed as goldsmiths and gold chain makers) came after the Napoleonic wars; and Jews arrived principally at the end of the nineteenth century.

Now a pleasant enough area in which to gaze at the amazing selection of jewellery displayed in the dozens of shop windows, Clerkenwell and Hatton Garden in earlier centuries were desperately poor, especially in Victorian times (indeed, Fagin's den was in Saffron Hill, a street which still exists, a few yards off Hatton Garden). The building of Holborn Viaduct, Farringdon Road and the underground gradually cleared away the slums. Today the area comprises lots of small roads criss-crossing one another, with the old buildings still occupied by hundreds of specialised workshops.

If you wish to trade in the family heirlooms, Hatton Garden is one place where you can get cash on the spot. But bullion dealers are not sentimental! No matter how fine the craftsmanship, or how gripping the history, the value of the item depends entirely on the quality and weight of the silver, gold or platinum. At the time of our visit, the international gold price (24 carat) was fixed at about £238 ($381) per troy ounce; the trade-in price for hall-marked 22 ct gold was just under £211. Krugerrands merited about £230, and sovereigns £53.

A visit to this area should be completed with a bite to eat from one of the many local sandwich bars (Jewish and Italian specialities abound) together with a shopping trip along Leather Lane, a market well known for its lunchtime bargains in clothing, hats, shoes, pot plants, bulbs and flowers.

Whether you are looking for a ring, bracelet, earrings, brooch, pendant, chain, cufflinks, watch, picture frame, snuff box, christening present, beads, gemstones, semi-precious stones or specialised tools, ... or wish to have your own design made up ... you have a tremendous choice. Some shops are well lit and upmarket; others less so. We are pleased to note that most shop windows display prices clearly. On our last visit, many shops offered discounts on the marked prices, and prices were obviously negotiable. The jewellery trade is an early victim of a recession; and one of the last markets to recover. It is generally accepted that prices are on average about 20% lower than in high street shops.

Many services are on offer: insurance valuations (at 1% of value), bead & pearl stringing (from £6 for a 16" necklace without knotting, or £10 for the same necklace with knotting), jewellery cleaning, engraving and repairs. If you take in your watch to be repaired anywhere in the country then there is a good chance that the work will be carried out in Clerkenwell.

The Factory Shop Guide for East Anglia & South-East England

70 London : Putney
Corcoran & May
157/161 Lower Richmond Road, SW15 1HH
(0181) 788 9556

Fabrics for curtains and furnishing. Top designers such as *Parkertex, GP & J Baker, Colefax & Fowler, Monkwell* and *Christian Fischbacher* all use Corcoran & May to dispose of seconds and overstocks. Thousands of metres available at any one time. Curtains and blinds made to measure.

'Many fabrics less than half recommended retail price. Average price £9.95.'

Open: Mon–Sat 10–5.30.
Closed: Bank Holidays; Christmas–New Year.
Cards: Access, Visa.
Cars: Side streets.
Toilets: Yes.
Wheelchairs: Two steps to medium shop.
Teas: Coffee shops nearby.
Transport: Putney Bridge tube, Putney BR station. bus no. 22.

....

Easy to see in the main road from Putney to Barnes.
(NB Lower Richmond Road is very long – you need the section nearer Putney, not near Richmond, and Mortlake cemetery.)
   From the south side of Putney bridge: take the road leading west along the Thames bank. Keep straight for 1/2 mile. Pass Shell petrol on the left then this double-fronted shop is on the left.

71 London : Wandsworth London
In-Wear
100 Garratt Lane SW18 4DI
(0181) 871 2155

Wide range of ladies' and men's fashion jackets, trousers, dresses, shirts, skirts, jeans etc., from the *In-Wear, Matinique* and *Part Two* collections.

'Samples, ends of lines and slightly imperfect merchandise.'

....

South of Wandsworth on A217, just off South Circular Rd (A205).
   From all directions: go to Wandsworth then go clockwise round one-way system. Pass town hall on right, staying in left lane. Go left at traffic lights (before Arndale Centre). Clearly marked company is 300 yds on right (beyond Sainsbury's on left). Go right into car-park.
   Coming north into Wandsworth on A217: look for clearly marked building on left, after the Old Sergeant pub on left.

Open: Mon–Fri 10–5; Sat 10–4.
Closed: Bank Holidays; Christmas–New Year.
Cards: Access, Amex, Transax, Visa.
Cars: Own car-park.
Toilets: Yes.
Wheelchairs: Easy access, no steps, large ground floor shop.
Changing rooms: Yes.
Teas: In the Arndale Centre.
Groups: Shopping groups welcome – please phone first.
Transport: Several buses, including nos. 35, 37, 44; 10 minutes' ride from Wandsworth Town Station.
Mail order: No.

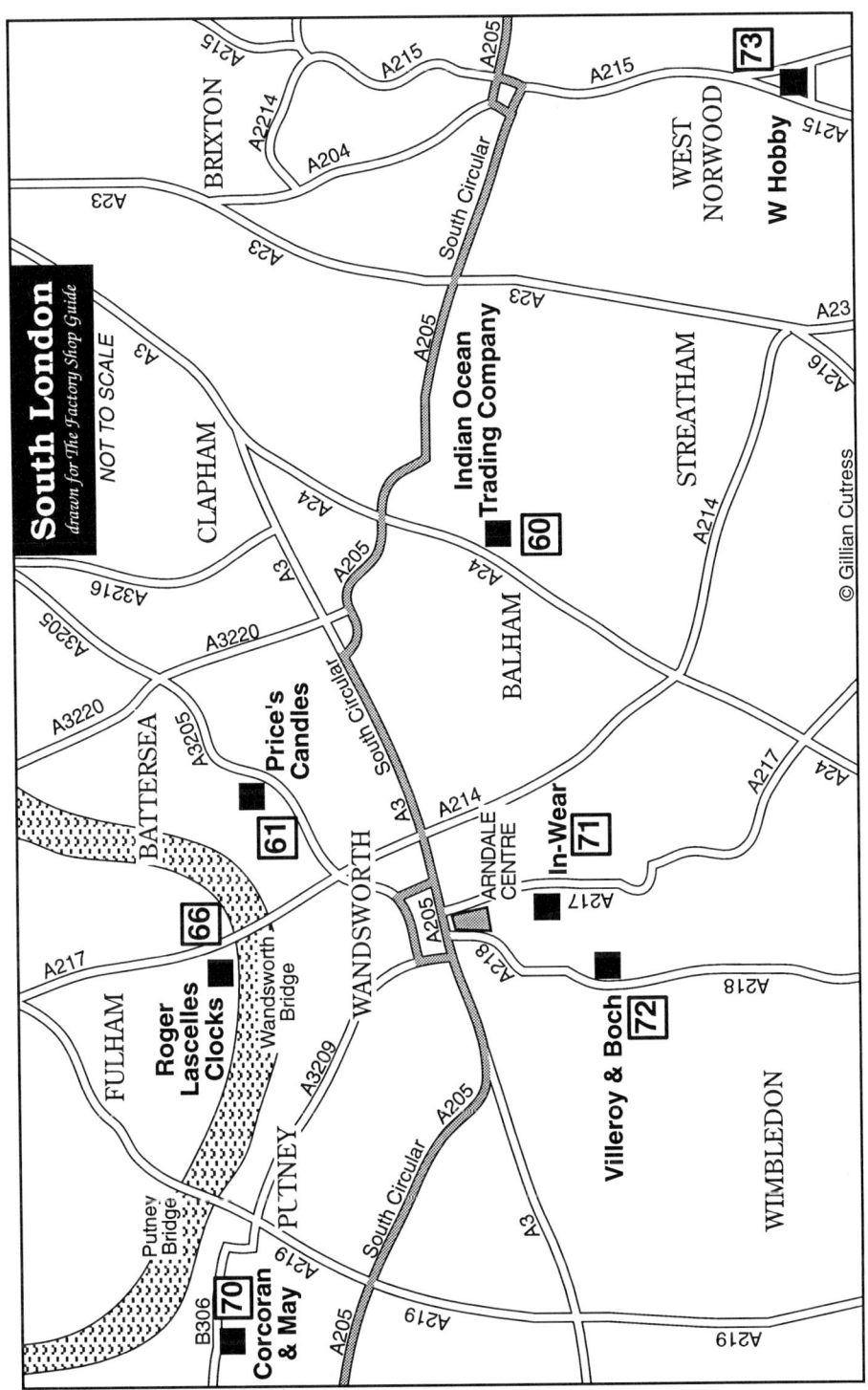

The Factory Shop Guide for East Anglia & South-East England

72 London : Wandsworth
Villeroy & Boch
267 Merton Road SW18 5JR
(0181) 870 4168

Large range of *Villeroy & Boch* china tableware, cookware, crystal glassware, gifts, cutlery etc.
'Discontinued stock, seconds, samples, perfects at reduced prices.'

....

South of Wandsworth on A218, just off South Circular Rd (A205).
   From all directions: go to Wandsworth then go clockwise round the one-way system. Pass town hall on right. Look for tall block of flats (Arndale Centre) ahead. Stay in left lane, go left after Arndale Centre. Continue for some distance along main road. Cross mini-roundabout, go over traffic lights. Shop in second building on left: large sign.
   Coming north into Wandsworth on Merton Road (A218) from South Wimbledon: look for this clearly signed building (set back from road) on the right, about 100 yds before traffic lights.

Open: Mon–Sat 10–5; some Sundays – please check.
Closed: Phone about Bank Holidays, Christmas.
Cards: Access, Amex, Diners, Switch, Visa.
Cars: Own car-park in front of building.
Toilets: No.
Wheelchairs: Ramp from car-park to large shop.
Teas: Locally.
Groups: No pottery tours. Shopping groups welcome; check with shop first.
Transport: Local buses; Southfields tube station half mile (District Line).

73 London : West Norwood
W Hobby Ltd *Knights Hill Square SE27* (0181) 761 4244

Huge selection of model kits: doll's houses and furniture, planes, boats, fairgrounds, trucks, carts, space cruisers, cathedrals etc. Musical movements; clocks. Candle kits. Modelling materials, balsa wood, paints, adhesives, moulds, plans, books. Power tools, soldering irons and accessories.
'Prices same as catalogue (but without postage). Reduced prices on some ex-catalogue items.'

....

Near West Norwood bus station.
   Via the South Circular (A205) from the west: at Tulse Hill go into the one-way system. *
   From Dulwich on S Circular (A205): go under railway in Thurlow Park Rd; pass Ford on left; at lights enter 1-way system. Keep left. *
   ***Exit for West/Upper Norwood** (White Hart Tavern on left, Gateway on right). Go under railway bridge, keep straight for 1/2 mile. Fork left (one-way system) beside huge stone church with clocktower and columns; go under railway bridge. Take second right (Langmead Street) then first left. Company straight ahead.
   From South Norwood/Croydon: go down Knight's Hill, pass Lambeth College on right. Go into one-way system. After repair shop/car sales, go right into Knight's Hill Square. Company ahead.

Open: Mon–Fri 9–5; Sat 9–1.
Closed: Bank Holidays.
Cards: Access, Eurocard, Switch, Visa.
Cars: Small car-park and on-street parking.
Toilets: Yes.
Wheelchairs: One tiny step to small shop.
Teas: Local pubs and cafés in West Norwood.
Groups: Model clubs please phone before visit.
Transport: West Norwood BR station. Local bus nos. 2b, 68 and 196.
Mail order: Yes.
Catalogue: 260 pages, £2.20. 24-hour ordering service for all items on (0181) 761 4247 by credit card. Gladly post overseas.

74 Luton Beds

Kangol Ltd.
46 Church Street LU1 3JC
(01582) 405000

Range of formal and casual hats for men and women; caps, berets, peak caps; handbags; some scarves.
'All hats are ends of ranges and slight seconds. Prices from about £2–£30.'

....

Facing the Arndale Shopping Centre in Luton centre.
   Coming into Luton from M1 exit 10: keep following signs to town centre. After traffic lights in town centre (large church on near left; multi-storey car-park on far left corner) company is on right, across dual carriageway, just before Herald & Post office and opposite Thrifty Car Rental. Best to follow signs into Market car-park on left.
   On foot from Arndale Centre: Church Street goes at right-angles around two sides of shopping precinct. Exit the Centre at sign for 'Church Street', look for large college opposite; go left down to traffic lights: shop facing you on far side of road.

Open: Mon–Fri 10–4; Sat 9–12.
Closed: Bank Holidays; Christmas, Boxing and New Year's Days.
Cards: Access, Visa.
Cars: Town car-parks. Nearest is Arndale Centre Market multi-storey.
Toilets: In Arndale Centre.
Wheelchairs: Shop on first floor up stairs.
Teas: In Arndale Centre.
Groups: Shoppers welcome with prior phone call. No factory tours.
Transport: 200 yds from bus station.

Hats and Luton

Bedfordshire had an established straw industry by the 1600's; in 1689 14,000 people in the Luton and Dunstable area derived their incomes from straw hats! Introduced by Flemish settlers, the country craft of straw plaiting flourished in private homes, the plaits being sent to Luton to be made into hats.

By the late 1700's, Italian straw hats were all the rage. But imported hats from Tuscany became unavailable – so the Luton quality improved, and employment, especially of women, increased greatly. Luton was the place where 'the women kept the men'. 'Plait schools' educated children in plaiting and weaving but not much else.

Imports from China and Japan, at one fifth of the price for an equal or better product, ruined the *plaiting* industry in the late 1800's. However this led to an improved *hat* industry as material costs were reduced. Sewing machines were used too.

After the first World War, felt ladies' hats became fashionable. The hat industry died elsewhere in this country but Luton and Dunstable manufacturing survived, not only of boaters but of cloth, felt and fur hats too. Today you can buy local boaters and, apparently, 'South American' panamas. Miniature boaters seen on dolls are produced here. If, like the author, you simply love hats, then you will enjoy the hat factory shop. Leave time to visit the local museum.

With thanks to the Luton Tourist Information Office (01582 401579) for details.

The Factory Shop Guide for East Anglia & South-East England

75 Midhurst W Sussex
Dexam International Ltd.
Holmbush Way, Holmbush Industrial Estate GU29 9HY
(01730) 814188

Wide range of *Chichester* stainless steel tableware (teapots, carving dishes etc), saucepans, stainless steel and cookware; glass, china, porcelain, Russian dolls, wooden boxes, gifts.
'Seconds and ends of ranges. All at exceptional prices.'
See display advertisement opposite.

....

On the south side of Midhurst.
From the centre of Midhurst: go south for Chichester. Go over mini-roundabout; keep going. After long left bend, go right in front of fire station (Holmbush Way). *
Coming north from Chichester (A286): as you reach Midhurst, look for fire station on left. Go left just after it, Holmbush Way. *
*Follow signs to Industrial Estate: bear left at mini roundabout, take second left at end of pine trees. Warehouse is at back left of cul-de-sac.

Open: Mon–Fri 10–3; Sat 10–1.
Closed: Bank Holidays; Christmas–New Year.
Cards: Access, Visa.
Cars: Plenty of space.
Toilets: Yes.
Wheelchairs: Large shop up flight of stairs on first floor (no lift).
Teas: Tea and coffee; cafés and pubs in Midhurst.
Groups: Shopping groups welcome if pre-arranged. Please phone.
Transport: 20 minutes' walk from town; bus no. 260 stops at fire station.

76 Norwich Norfolk
The Bally Factory Shop
Hall Road NR32 2LM (NEW) *(01603) 760590*

Large range of ladies', men's and children's footwear. Handbags and accessories.
'Factory shop in factory complex.'

....

Near southern edge of town.
The A47 (Kings Lynn–Great Yarmouth dual carriageway) forms the southern bypass of Norwich.
From the A47, B1108 B1172 and A11: stay on or turn onto A47 for Great Yarmouth and then turn off onto the A140 for Norwich. *
From Great Yarmouth on A47 and Beccles on A146: stay on or turn onto A47 towards Kings Lynn. Then turn off onto A140 towards Norwich. *
From Ipswich on A140: go underneath A47 southern bypass. *
*Turn right immediately after the Lex Ford garage on right. **
From town centre and northerly directions: go to or around inner ring road and turn onto A140 for Ipswich. 2 miles from city centre turn left immediately after the Forte Posthouse on left. **
**Pass Toyota, Nissan and Peugeot on right: after 200 yds go right in front of bollards into Bally's car-park.

Open: Mon–Fri 9.30–5.30; Sat 9–5.30. Most Bank Holidays – phone first to check.
Closed: Christmas, Boxing and New Year's Days.
Cards: Access, Amex, Barclaycard, Diners Club, Connect, Switch.
Cars: Ample free parking outside shop.
Toilets: Yes, and for disabled.
Wheelchairs: Ramp for easy access to huge shop.
Teas: Coffee shop for coffee, tea, cold drinks, light lunches, cream teas.
Groups: No factory tours but shopping groups and coaches always welcome by prior arrangement. Contact Sally Jackson or Debbie Wicks.
Transport: Cityline bus no. 11 stops virtually opposite.

Stainless steel "Chichester" teapots, carving dishes and trays. **Kitchen** jugs, cook's jars, kettles, potato bakers, cook's knives and chopping boards, graters, casseroles, copper flambé dishes, frying pans, steamer sets, sauté pans, colanders, buckets, preserving pans, **Stainless steel** saucepans and roasting tins, trays, fondue and wok sets. **Glassware** drinking glasses and decanters. **Kids' ware** cuddly toys Russian dolls, wooden birds. **Chinese** rice bowls, dishes and chopsticks. **Porcelain** ornamental figurines. **Stationery** greeting cards, writing and wrapping materials. **Giftware** ashtrays, photo frames, money boxes, miniature Cloisonne teapots and eggs, vases, bowls, candles and candlesticks, baskets. **China tableware** cutlery, plates and dishes, teapots, cups and mugs, condiment sets.

Our Factory Shops are real Aladdin's Caves!

We make all our stainless steel products in our Chichester factory and we import many types of goods.
This alllows us to have such a wide range of products.
Our two shops offer seconds or discontinued items at greatly reduced prices.

Chichester
Goodwood Metalcraft Ltd
Terminus Rd Ind Est.
Chichester
01243 537956

Shops open Mon–Fri 10am – 3pm
and Sat 10am – 1pm

Midhurst
Dexam International
Holmbush Way Ind Est.
Midhurst
01730 814188

See our entries nos 21 and 76

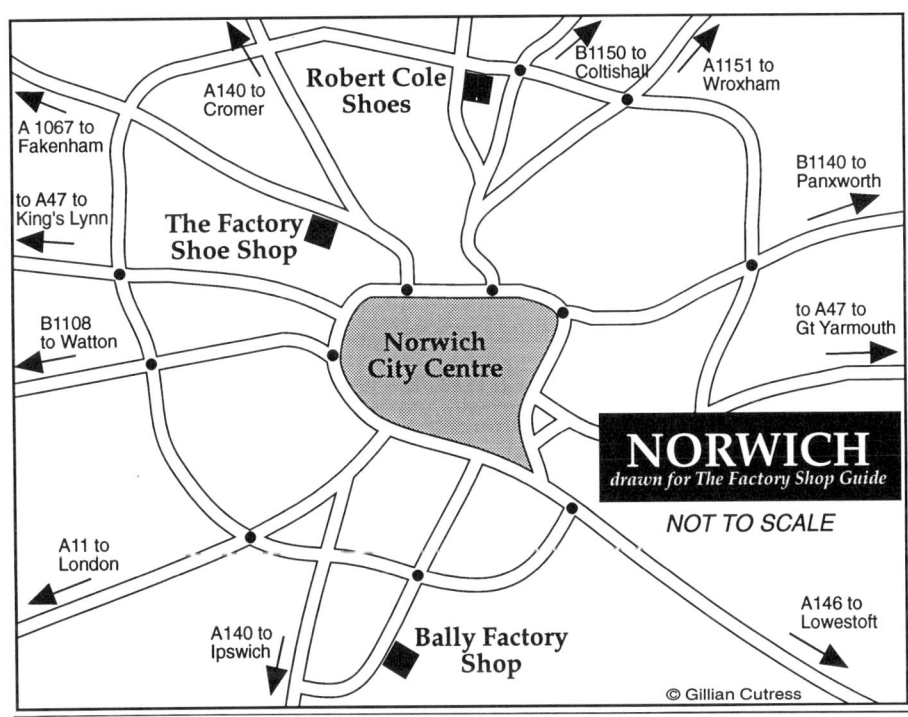

The Factory Shop Guide for East Anglia & South-East England

77 Norwich Norfolk
Country House Flowers
Washingford House, Bergh Apton NR15 1AA
(01508) 550469

Large selection of everything for the dried flower enthusiast including unusual arrangements. Commissions happily undertaken. Most flowers grown on the farm.
'Bridal work to order. Tuition – small groups by arrangement. All at very reasonable prices.'

See display advertisement opposite.

....

Bergh Apton is a small villlage 7 miles south-east of Norwich, just off A146.
   From Norwich: take A146 for Lowestoft. After 5 miles pass Yelverton Car Sales; take first right, then next left; go on for 1/2 mile: Washingford House is on left, opposite post office.
   From the south-east: in Thurton go left at the George and Dragon pub and immediately bear right. After 1/2 mile turn right, go on for 1 mile: Washingford House is on right, opposite post office.

Open: Mon–Fri 2–4; Sun and Bank Holidays 2–4.
Closed: Saturdays; Good Friday; Christmas–New Year.
Cards: No.
Cars: Outside shop.
Toilets: Yes.
Wheelchairs: One step to small shop.
Teas: Happy to put on kettle for weary customers! Cafés in Loddon and Norwich.
Groups: Small pre-booked groups welcome.
Transport: None.
Mail order: No.

78 Norwich Norfolk
The Factory Shoe Shop
Esdelle Works, Drayton Road NR3 4RP
(01603) 425907

Ladies' and men's quality footwear from own Norwich factories and associated continental factories. Slim to wide fittings usually in stock. Brands include Van-Dal, Holmes, Jenny and Gallus. Also stock quality handbags.
'Over 4,000 pairs of slight seconds and ends of ranges at reduced prices.'

....

About 3/4 mile north-west of inner ring road (A147).
   From large roundabout on St Crispin's Road (inner ring road): turn off due north into Pitt Street (A140 and A1067), for 'Swimming Pool, Cromer, Fakenham'; after 1/2 mile, fork left into Drayton Rd (A1067); pass Wensum Park. Factory on left; shop 50 yds down drive past factory.
   From north-west section of outer ring road (A140): at traffic lights by Asda, go into Drayton Road (A1067) for city centre. Go over large roundabout, look for Wickes DIY on right; shop is just beyond, on right, down drive before factory, well marked.

Open: Mon–Sat 10–4.
Closed: Bank Holidays; Christmas–New Year.
Cards: Access, Switch, Visa.
Cars: Own large car-park.
Toilets: Nearby.
Wheelchairs: No steps to large shop.
Teas: Many places in Norwich.
Groups: Shopping groups welcome; book with Mrs Green and ask for discount details. For factory tour call Personnel on (01603) 426341.
Transport: Cityline bus no. 11 stops outside.
Mail order: No.

COUNTRY HOUSE FLOWERS

Dried Flower Farm Shop

Open 2 – 4 daily (Not Saturday)

Superb arrangements and everything for the dried flower enthusiast.

Group visits welcome.

Tuition by arrangement.

Tel (01508) 550469
Washingford House, Bergh Apton
(opposite the Post Office)
6 miles S.E. of Norwich off A146.

79 Norwich Norfolk

Robert Cole Shoes
90 Catton Grove Road
NR3 3AB
(01603) 487757

Shoes from local, UK and worldwide factories. Over 4,000 shoes on display in all makes, sizes, styles and colours. Major brands, chainstore seconds, discontinued lines, samples.
'The quality footwear discount shop of East Anglia. All stock sold at very competitive prices. Men's shoes from £13–£60; ladies' shoes from £8–£60; children's shoes from £6–£30.'

....

On the northern section of the main Norwich ring road between the Cromer Road (A140) and the North Walsham Road (B1150). Shop is clearly visible at junction of Catton Grove Road and the ring road.

Open: Mon–Sat 9–5.30; Sun 10.30–4.30; Bank Holidays.
Closed: Christmas and Boxing Days.
Cards: Access, Visa.
Cars: Own well signposted car-park.
Toilets: No.
Wheelchairs: One step.
Teas: In Norwich.
Groups: Shopping groups please book first with Robert Cole or Denise West.
Transport: Several local buses stop outside door.
Mail order: Yes.
Catalogue: No.

80 Papworth Everard Cambs
Papworth Travel Goods
CB3 8RC
(01480) 830345

Range of top-quality leather travel goods, briefcases and suitcases.
'Seconds and discontinued lines only.'

....

Easy to find, on the A1198 (Huntingdon–Royston road) about 6 miles south of Huntingdon and 11 miles west of Cambridge.
There is only one road through this village. Shop is next to the park and beside the pedestrian lights. Follow signs to car-park. Shop entrance is through reception.

Open: Mon–Thur 8.30–12.30 and 1.30–5; Fri 8.30–11.30.
Closed: Bank Holidays; Spring Bank Holiday week; first 2 weeks in August, Christmas–New Year.
Cards: Access, Amex, Visa.
Cars: Outside reception.
Toilets: Yes.
Wheelchairs: No access to upstairs showroom.
Teas: Local pubs or Little Chef.
Groups: No factory tours.
Transport: Hourly buses from Cambridge and St Ives.
Mail order: Yes.
Catalogue: Yes. Free. Seconds and discontinued lines only.

81 Peterborough Cambs
Jaeger Sale Shop
3 Cumbergate PE1 1YS
(01733) 63114

Previous season's Jaeger ladies' collection from UK and export. *'All stock perfect but one season behind. Sales twice yearly for extra bargains. Ask to go on mailing list, mentioning this book.'*

....

In the town centre.
From A1: take A605 into Peterborough. Pass Rover garage on left, go over railway; go left at roundabout on to A15. Cross river and stay on A15, for Sleaford/Lincoln. At large roundabout with footbridges over it, go into Queensgate Shopping Centre car-park.*
Via A47 from Leicester or Wisbech: turn on to A15 for Peterborough Centre; go into Queensgate Shopping Centre car-park opposite station.*
*Go down to ground floor of car-park and walk almost to end: go right into Cumbergate. Jaeger shortly on right.

Open: Mon–Sat 9.30–5.30.
Closed: Bank Holidays; Christmas, Boxing and New Year's Days.
Cards: Access, Amex, Diners, Jaeger Credit Card, Visa.
Cars: In town centre.
Toilets: No.
Wheelchairs: Wheelchairs can be collected from 11th floor of Queensgate car-park – book first to ensure availability.
Changing rooms: Yes.
Teas: Hot and cold drinks willingly made! Toy box for children.
Groups: Shopping groups welcome – phone call appreciated.
Transport: In town centre; near bus and train stations.
Mail order: No.

82 Peterborough Cambs
Stage 2 (Freemans)
Saville Road PE3 7PP
(01733) 263308

All ranges from Freemans' catalogue including men's, ladies' and children's clothing, household items & electrical goods.
'All items at greatly reduced prices.'

....

Opposite Driving Test Centre north-west of city centre.
   From A1: take A605 into Peterborough; pass Rover garage on left, go over railway, turn left at roundabout on to A15; cross river; stay on A15 to Sleaford and Lincoln. After large Toys R Us go left over railway then right at next two roundabouts. Go left at T-junction; Stage 2 clearly signed on left.
   Via A47 from Leicester/Wisbech: turn on to A15 for Peterborough Centre; go right at second roundabout, go over railway, turn right at next two roundabouts. Go left at T-junction; Stage 2 clearly signed on left.

Open: Mon–Fri 10–8; Sat 8–6. Please phone about Bank Holidays.
Closed: Christmas–New Year.
Cards: Access, Visa.
Cars: Own large car-park.
Toilets: No.
Wheelchairs: Easy access to very large shop.
Changing rooms: Yes.
Teas: In town.
Groups: Coach parties welcome; but please phone to arrange time.
Transport: Not easy.
Mail order: No.
Catalogue: No.

83 Rayleigh Essex
Falmer Jeans Ltd.
24–26 Brook Road SS6 7XF
(01268) 773633

Wide range of men's and ladies' jeans and casual wear: shorts, T-shirts, blouses etc.
'All items are ends of lines, previous year's ranges or slightly substandard stock at reduced prices.'

....

On south side of Rayleigh, just off Southend Arterial Road (A127).
   Going east on A127 to Southend: go left at Rayleigh Weir overpass/roundabout. At huge roundabout, take second left (The Weir pub on left) as if going back on to A127.*
   From Southend on A127: go to major roundabout as above, then double back as if going back along dual carriageway.*
   *Take first left, following signs to Industrial estate; go right into Brook Road. Company clearly marked on right.

Open: Mon–Sat 9–5.30. Phone for Bank Holidays. Some days between Christmas–New Year.
Closed: Some Bank Holidays.
Cards: Access, Switch, Visa.
Cars: Outside shop.
Toilets: Ask if necessary.
Wheelchairs: Assistance into sizeable shop by prior arrangement.
Changing rooms: Yes.
Teas: In Rayleigh.
Groups: Shopping groups welcome if they phone first.
Transport: Buses to Rayleigh Weir then 1/4 mile walk.
Mail order: No.

The Factory Shop Guide for East Anglia & South-East England

84 Romford Essex

Hubbinet Reproductions
Unit 7, Hubbinet Ind. Estate, Eastern Avenue West   RM7 7NV
(01708) 762212

Maker of quality traditional & reproduction furniture in hand finished mahogany and yew wood veneer. Over 100 models of bookcases (from £80), library bookcases (from £500), dining sets (from £600), desks, bureaux, TV, hi-fi and video units (from £200), occasional tables. Advice on furnishings.
'Factory seconds and export rejects at up to 50% off. Modify & colour to customers' requirements. January, April, Nov sales.'
See display advertisement opposite.
....

Off the A12 north of Romford.
   From London on A12: cross A1112 at traffic lights. After a mile cross another set of traffic lights, then pass Mercedes garage and take first left.*
   From M25 exit 28: aim for London on A12. At Gallows Corner (flyover/big roundabout) stay on A12. After 2 miles pass MFI and BAC on left then make U-turn at next traffic lights. After Mercedes garage take first left.*
   *Pass Falconcraft on left then go into next industrial estate on left. Inside, turn left and follow signs.

Open: Mon–Fri 9–5; Sat 10–4; Sun phone for information.
Closed: 24 Dec–10 Jan.
Cards: Visa, Access.
Cars: Easy, outside shop.
Toilets: Yes.
Wheelchairs: No steps.
Teas: Sandwiches and cold drinks at nearby garage.
Transport: Romford BR station then bus to Eastern Avenue; Newbury Park underground station on Central Line. Then no. 66 or Eastern National bus to Parkside, Romford.

85 Royston Herts

The Shoe Shed
Orchard Road SG8 5HB
(01763) 241933

Thousands of pairs of men's, ladies' and children's shoes, all perfects.
'One of UK's largest footwear distributors – shoes bought in from UK and all over world. Current perfect merchandise at competitive prices (many reduced by about 30%): ladies' shoes, sandals from £5, men's from £10.'
....

Located within Clothing World, on the Royston Industrial Estate, near the railway station.
   Going into Royston on the A505: get onto the Royston by-pass following the signs to station/industrial estate. Passing Tesco, go straight over two roundabouts, then take third turning on right (Orchard Road), then first on left.
   Coming into Royston on the A10: go through town, following signs to Station; pass station on left, take second turning on left into Orchard Road, then turn first left.

Open: Tues–Wed 9–5.30; Thur–Fri 9–6; Sat 9–4; Sun 10–2.
Closed: Mondays; Christmas and Boxing Day.
Cards: No.
Cars: Free parking available.
Toilets: No.
Wheelchairs: The Shoe Shed is located on the 1st floor. Staff are willing to take stock to customers on ground floor, which they can select from a catalogue.
Teas: No.
Groups: No.
Transport: 5 minutes' walk from station; 15 mins from town centre. Bus nos.16 and 17 (not Sundays).

Hubbinet Reproductions

Everything we sell is manufactured on the premises at only a little over half the price you would pay in a quality store!

Beautiful hand finished reproduction furniture in mahogany and yew wood finishes. Also exclusive collectors pieces It's worth your while to pay us a visit!

Open all week and Saturdays

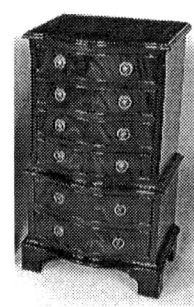

Unit 7, Hubbinet Industrial Estate, Eastern Avenue West
Romford RM7 7NU
Tel (01708) 762212
Fax (01708) 766511

---

86 Rye E Sussex

Rye Pottery
Ferry Road TN31 7DJ
(01797) 223363

Wide range of decorated earthenware: some mugs, dishes, cake stands; selection of dogs, cats, owls, hares etc plus collector's range of figures from Chaucer's Canterbury Tales and American Folk Heroes.

'Perfects; and seconds reduced by 33%. Mail order service for firsts only. Please mention this book when requesting catalogue. Special commissions accepted.'

On the west side of Rye.
   By car: go round town till you see signs to 'Battle B2089' then follow them; go over level crossing; pottery is in large detached house 200 yds on right, just past The Ferry Boat Inn.
   By train then foot: turn right outside station, go to end of road, turn right; go over level crossing; pottery is in large detached house 200 yds on right, just past The Ferry Boat Inn.
   From Battle on B2089: go down Udimore Hill into Rye, pass the 'Cinque Ports' sign, then pottery is just over 1/2 mile on left, just before The Ferry Boat Inn.

Open: Mon–Fri 9–12 & 2–5; Sat 9.30–12.30 & 2.30–5.
Closed: Bank Holidays; Christmas–New Year.
Cards: Access, Visa.
Cars: 2 car spaces beside pottery; town car-parks and local streets.
Toilets: In town.
Wheelchairs: Five steps and cobbled path so not possible for wheelchairs.
Teas: Lots of places in Rye.
Groups: No.
Transport: 5 minutes' walk from station.
Mail order: Yes.
Catalogue: Yes. Free. No seconds sent.

The Factory Shop Guide for East Anglia & South-East England

87 Saffron Walden — Essex
Swaine Adeney Brigg
Nursery Road, Great Chesterford CB10 1QV
(01799) 530521

Luxury country clothing: ladies' and men's tailored jackets, trousers, skirts, jumpers, blouses, shirts, scarves, gloves and wax and cotton outerwear; English bridle hide leathergoods; gifts, toiletries and the famous *Brigg* umbrella.

'Perfect ends of lines etc. Usually at least 30% off London retail prices.'

Open: Tues–Sat 10.30–4.
Closed: Monday; Good Friday; Christmas–New Year.
Cards: Access, Amex, Switch, Visa.
Cars: Factory car park.
Toilets: Yes.
Wheelchairs: One step to small shop.
Changing rooms: Yes.
Teas: Gluttons Café in Saffron Walden.
Transport: Great Chesterford BR station behind factory.
Mail order: No.

About 4 miles north-west of Saffron Walden and near M11 exit 9.

Going north on M11: take exit 9 (for A11 Norwich). At first roundabout (junction with A1301 for Sawston and Cambridge, and B184 for Saffron Walden) take exit for Saffron Walden.*

Going south on M11: take exit 10 then A505 towards Sawston. After 1 1/2 miles turn right on to A1301 for Saffron Walden. At roundabout with A11, take B184 for Saffron Walden.*

*At roundabout go right for Great Chesterford. Continue around sweeping left bend, pass glass house (nursery) on right and turn right immediately. Shop is at the end, straight ahead.

88 Seaford — E Sussex
Sheban Furniture Ltd.
Cradle Hill Ind Est BN25 3JF
(01323) 891710

Fine reproduction furniture in mahogany, yew and burr elm wood veneer finishes. All pieces are hand-finished. Models available are bookcases, bureaux, desks, dining suites, bedroom furniture and occasional pieces.

'Save up to 40% on high street prices when buying directly from this maker. Delivery service available: for small items, a charge of £25 is made; for larger purchases, 6% of the value of the purchase.' See display advertisement opposite.

Open: Mon–Fri 10–5; Sat 10–1.
Closed: 23 Dec–8 Jan.
Cards: Access, Visa.
Cars: Own car-park.
Toilets: Yes.
Wheelchairs: No steps to shop.
Teas: In Seaford; attractive country pubs in area.
Transport: Short taxi ride from Seaford BR station.

In industrial estate at north-east edge of town.

From Brighton and town centre on A259: go towards Eastbourne on the A259. About half a mile from town centre turn left following sign to Alfriston.*

From Eastbourne on A259: pass Esso petrol station on left; after about 30 yds go right towards Alfriston, also Drusilla's Zoo Park (brown sign).*

*After nearly half a mile turn left immediately before the cemetery on left. Shop is about 300 yds on right.

SHEBAN
FURNITURE LTD

Fine reproduction furniture in hand finished mahogany, yew and burr elm wood finishes.

Discontinued lines & slight imperfects available at all times.

Cradle Hill Industrial Estate
Seaford, East Sussex BN25 3JE
Tel (01323) 891710 Fax (01323) 893748

---

89 Sevenoaks Kent

Corcoran & May
1 St Botolph's Road TN13 3AK
(0732) 741851

Fabrics for curtains and furnishing. Top designers such as *Parkertex, GP & J Baker, Colefax & Fowler, Monkwell* and *Christian Fischbacher* all use Corcoran & May to dispose of seconds and overstocks. Thousands of metres available at any one time. Curtains and blinds made to measure.

'Many fabrics less than half recommended retail price. Average price £9.95.'

....

Open: Mon–Sat 10–5.30.
Closed: Bank Holidays; Christmas–New Year.
Cards: Access, Visa.
Cars: Street parking nearby (double lines immediately outside).
Toilets: Yes.
Wheelchairs: No steps to medium sized shop.
Teas: Lots of tea shops in town.
Transport: Any train or bus to town.

Easy to find on the north side of town, 100 yds from the station.
   From the M25/north: aim for Sevenoaks centre. Pass the station on your right.*
      *From the station: go uphill; pass the Railway & Bicycle pub on right; shop is on next near left corner.
   From the south/Hildenborough: go into town, pass Knowle House (NT) on right; fork left for Dunton Green/London/M25. Go through town and downhill. Pass Jaguar showroom on right; after several hundred yards, shop is clearly visible on far right corner.

The Factory Shop Guide for East Anglia & South-East England

90 Sheerness, Isle of Sheppey Kent
B & A Whelan
52 High Street, Blue Town ME12 1RV
(01795) 663879

Huge selection of concrete garden ornaments made here. Houses, wells, urns, troughs, pots, gnomes, cupids, wheelbarrows, bird baths, sundials, animals, pedestals, seats etc.
'Family run business, over 600 designs. Always some reduced prices. The UK's largest concrete ornament manufacturer.'

....

Go over bridge on to Isle of Sheppey. At first roundabout go left, then keep following signs to Sheerness Docks. Cross industrial railway crossing by steel mill then take third left.

Open: Seven days a week 9–6.
Closed: Christmas–New Year.
Cards: None.
Cars: Own car-park.
Toilets: Yes.
Wheelchairs: Easy access, huge outdoor show area.
Teas: Great variety of fish and chip shops, Chinese and Indian restaurants and pubs in Sheerness.
Groups: Shopping groups welcome. No guided tours.
Transport: 10 minutes' walk from railway and bus stations.
Mail order: No.

91 Shoreham-by-Sea W Sussex
Claremont Garments
26 Dolphin Road BN43 6PR
(01273) 461571

Ladies' and girls' underwear and nightwear; ladies' and children's outerwear. Increased range of stock.
'Seconds and ends of lines sold here including chainstore items.'

....

From M23/Brighton: drive along seafront through Portslade and Southwick into Shoreham. Pass B&Q and Halfords on right; go right at traffic lights after Courts.*

From Worthing on coast road (A259): at roundabout go right for Shoreham town centre; drive through Shoreham. Pass large Esso petrol station on right then go left at traffic lights for Dolphin Industrial Estate.*

*Cross level crossing, go right into Dolphin Road (parallel to railway); well marked building (Deyong Golding sign) on left. Go up drive on left.

Open: Mon–Thur 9.15–4.30; Fri 10–1. Phone to check.
Closed: Bank Holidays; 1 week at Whitsun (phone for dates); last 2 weeks August; Christmas–New Year. Phone to confirm.
Cards: No.
Cars: Own car-park.
Toilets: Ask if desperate!
Wheelchairs: Showroom on first floor (no lift).
Changing rooms: No.
Teas: Welcome to use factory canteen (8–2pm).
Groups: Welcome to shop, but essential to phone Sue Cush first.
Transport: 10 minutes' walk from centre of Shoreham.

The Factory Shop Guide for East Anglia & South-East England

92 Sittingbourne Kent

Michelsons
Staplehurst Road ME10 2NI
(01795) 426821

Top quality men's wear: neckties and bow ties (also for clubs and companies); cravats, cummerbunds, silk hankies; shirts – formal, dress, casual and leisure; waistcoats; leather belts; braces; boxer shorts etc.

'All items perfect, ends of ranges etc. Some items up to 50% off. Silk ties from £10; shirts from £15. Men's leather belts from £15, all perfect samples.'

....

To the west of Sittingbourne.
   From town centre: take A2 westwards for London. Pass Fina petrol station on left then go right into Staplehurst Road in front of Esso petrol station. *
   From the A2 coming into town from Gillingham or M2 exit 5: after large Esso petrol station on left (pedestrian crossing in front) go left into Staplehurst Road. *
   ***Pass Murco petrol station, go over railway, turn left into company drive: clearly marked shop.**

Open: Mon–Thur 9–4; Fri 9–12. Some Saturdays before Christmas – please phone to check.
Closed: Bank Holidays; Christmas–New Year.
Cards: No.
Cars: Own large car-park for cars and coaches.
Toilets: No.
Wheelchairs: 2 small steps.
Changing rooms: No.
Teas: Staff canteen or in Sittingbourne.
Tours: Pre-booked half hour factory tours Mon–Thur at 10.45 and 1.45. For tours and shopping groups please contact John Brown, mentioning this book.
Mail order: No.

93 Slough Berks

Mexx Factory Outlet
132 Fairlie Road, Slough Trading Estate SL1 4PV
(01753) 525450

Huge range of men's, ladies', kids' and teens' fashion clothing – sweatshirts, jeans, shorts, T-shirts, skirts etc. All standard ranges plus a few samples.

'All first quality, previous season's items and some samples. Substantial discounts on previous high street prices. Ask to go on mailing list for special sales. Factory outlet information line for current promotions.'

....

On the huge and well-marked Slough Trading Estate, north-west of Slough.
   From M4 exit 6: go towards Slough then follow signs to Trading Estate. At traffic lights (Office World on near left, Do-It-All on far left) go left (Buckingham Avenue). At second traffic lights go right then continue to clearly marked company on right. Car-park and entrance at back.

Open: Mon–Sat 9.30–5.30 (Thur late night to 7); Sun 10–4.
Closed: Phone to check Christmas–New Year.
Cards: Access, Connect, Switch, Visa.
Cars: Own car-park at rear.
Toilets: Yes.
Wheelchairs: No steps to vast shop.
Changing rooms: Yes.
Teas: Vending machine for cold drinks in seating area.
Groups: Shopping groups of all sizes welcome. Children's play, drawing and competition area with television.

The Factory Shop Guide for East Anglia & South-East England

94 Stanton near Bury St Edmunds Suffolk
Playdri Products Ltd.
Shepherd's Grove Industrial Estate IP31 2AP
(01359) 251420

Waterproof suits, windcheaters, casual jackets. Golf shoes, bags, balls, golf trollies, travel bags, clubs etc.
'Sales at Easter and in November. Phone for exact dates.'

....

11 miles north-east of Bury St Edmunds, 12 miles south-west of Diss.
   From Bury: take A143 north-east. In Stanton, just after Esso garage on left, go right into Stanton village. Pass church and war memorial on right. After 150 yds go right for industrial estate. *
   From Diss: go south on A143. Turn left for Shepherd's Grove Ind. Est. West. Keep following signs to this estate, turning left. *
   *Pass school on right and windmill on left. Go left into Grove Lane. Continue round road for 2/3 mile; go right to estate; take first left; at end of lane go right. Clearly visible factory 300 yds on right, set back.

Open: Mon–Fri 9–4.30.
Closed: Bank Holidays, and near a sale (ie, closed week before Easter and week in November).
Cards: Access, Visa.
Cars: Outside factory.
Toilets: Yes.
Wheelchairs: Rather restricted movement within shop.
Changing rooms: No.
Teas: 1/2 mile up Grove Lane.
Groups: Shopping groups welcome, but please telephone first.
Transport: None.
Mail order: No.

95 Sudbury Suffolk
Vanners Mill Shop
Gregory Street CO10 6BC   *(01787) 313933*

Silk fabric by the metre. Wide range of articles in silk, woven here or printed at company's Crayford mill, eg scarves, boxer shorts, ties, handkerchiefs, purses, wallets etc.
'Most items perfect but some fabric slightly substandard. All at mill shop prices. Many bargains in firsts and famous name seconds. From £2.50 per metre for pure silk. For special sale dates, ring (01322) 559401, mentioning this book.'

....

Easy to find in middle of town (large one-way system).
   From Market Square: go clockwise (Midland Bank on left). *
   From other directions: follow road round for Bury St Edmunds (A134). *
   *After junction where A131 goes left to Chelmsford, keep clockwise on A131 (A134) for Bury. Clearly marked mill 100 yds on right (before fire station on left).
   From Chelmsford on A131: you must go left onto one-way system as you reach town. Shop 100 yds on right.
   From Bury St Edmunds on A134: go into town, take first turn for Chelmsford (A131) then A134 back towards Bury as above.

Open: Mon–Fri 9–5; Sat 9–12.
Closed: Bank Holidays; Christmas–New Year.
Cards: Access, Visa.
Cars: Car-park opposite, beside fire station.
Toilets: In factory – ask if desperate!
Wheelchairs: No steps to expanded showroom.
Teas: Lots of places in town.
Groups: No mill tours. Shopping groups always welcome – prior phone call, please.
Transport: Any bus to town then short walk.

Silk in Suffolk & Essex

Records show that a fledgling silk industry existed in Suffolk, with workers who had moved out from Spitalfields in London, in 1793. By 1840 the main locations were Sudbury, with 600 looms and Haverhill with some 60. Specialities here were parasol silks; while black silk crêpes for mourning were made by Samuel Courtauld, and high quality furnishing fabrics by Mr Warner, in Braintree. Mr Vanner opened his first 'factory' (a warehouse to serve handloom weavers) in 1871 but unfortunately from that time onwards there was almost uninterrupted decline of the English silk industry, first in face of French competition and later from man-made fabrics.

Nationally, numbers employed tumbled from 130,000 in 1851 to under 30,000 in 1907. Like the straw hat industry (*see p. 59*) two or three times as many women as men were employed but wages were poor by any standard at that period. In 1886, men earned 23/- [£1.15] weekly and women a meagre 10/4d [51.2p]. The operatives worked in their own homes as Sudbury's first power loom factory was not built until 1896.

You can still see examples of three-storey cottages in Sudbury with long windows on the middle floor to allow maximum light on the looms.

Warners of Braintree closed in 1971. Richard Humphries, who became the last textile designer for Jacquard weaving at Warners, salvaged the ancient machinery as the mill was cleared for scrap, and began his own weaving company in Sudbury. He then expanded to Devere Mill in nearby Castle Hedingham and in 1975 opened the doors to the public.

Over the next few years, other local mills closed, thus enabling Richard Humphries to salvage more machines. Devere Mill became overcrowded with both machinery and visitors, so, in the interest of maintaining a representation of the East Anglian silk trade, the local council began a £3.5 million restoration of the original Warners Mill at Braintree, now known as 'New Mills'. This had been built between 1808 and 1860 by the Walters family, an earlier generation of Huguenot descendants. In 1990, almost 20 years after the looms had originally been taken from this building, Richard Humphries was able to move them back.

New Mills now houses The Working Silk Museum, where visitors can see ten of the original hand looms in daily use and learn how exquisite silk designs are produced, using the thousands of hand cut Jacquard cards. The exhibition area includes a large display of fine silks.

The Working Silk Museum in Braintree: mill & shop Mon–Fri 10-12.30 & 1.30–5; shop only: Sat 1.30–5. Guided tours Mon–Fri 2, 3 and 4pm. Phone (01376) 553393.

If you wish to see silk printed and to learn more about this fine fabric, visit David Evans (p. 21) (the sister company of Vanners) in Crayford, Kent.

With thanks to Vanners for providing information

The Factory Shop Guide for East Anglia & South-East England

96 Tiptree   Essex
The Factory Shop
The Crossroads CO5 7VW
(01621) 817662

Large selection of men's, ladies' and children's clothing, footwear, luggage, toiletries, hardware, household textiles, gifts, bedding, lighting, Wrangler and Eastex departments, and new fashion concessions department with famous brand names.

'Large stock of chainstore items, all at greatly reduced prices.'

....

In the middle of Tiptree by the crossing of the B1022 and the B1023.
   From the north (on B1023): the shop is on the right just by the crossing with B1022.
   From the south: pass the windmill (no sails) and Burmah petrol station on right, and the shop is on far left corner of the crossing.

Open: Mon–Fri 9.30–5; Sat 9–5; Sun 11–5.
Closed: Bank Holidays; Christmas, Boxing and New Year's Days.
Cards: Access, Switch, Visa.
Cars: Own large car-park.
Toilets: In town.
Wheelchairs: No steps.
Changing rooms: Yes.
Teas: Cafés and pubs in town.
Groups: Glad to see shopping groups – prior phone call appreciated.
Transport: Bus service from Clacton to Maldon. Bus stop outside.
Mail order: No.

With thanks to the shops who kindly allowed us to take photographs or who supplied them to us ...

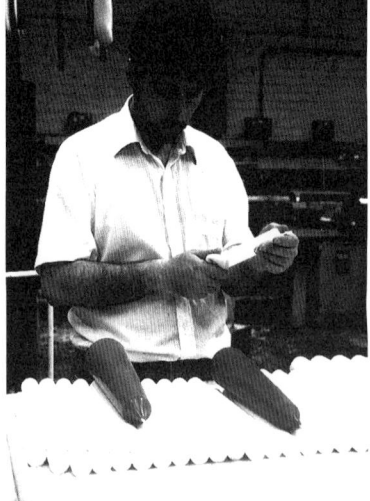

p.6   Exteriors of factory shops:
        Peter Newman;
        Price's Candles;
        The Wilky Group;
        The Table Place;
        Sheban Furniture;
        Carpet Bags;
        Merchants Quay.
p. 23 Cutting leather: Nursey & Son.
p. 27 Printing silk: David Evans.
         Smoking fish: The Weald Smokery.
p. 74 Candle manufacture: Price's Candles.
p. 93 Clothes from M&G Fashions;
        clock from Roger Lascelles;
         flowers from Essentially Hops;
        Mascot countrywear;
        decorations from Price's Candles;
        wine cooler from Henry Watson's Potteries.

Royal Scot Crystal Factory Shop

Poplars Nursery Garden Centre
Harlington Road
Toddington
LU5 6HE
(01525) 875897
Open 7 days 10–5

97 Toddington Beds

Royal Scot Crystal
Poplars Nursery, Harlington Road LU5 6HF
(01525) 875897

Hand-cut lead crystal glasses, decanters, vases etc. Specially engraved items. Crystal animals, paperweights and perfume bottles. Golf prizes.

'Most items made in own factory (not at this location). Sell first quality, some seconds and discontinued lines at substantially reduced prices.'

See display advertisement above.

Open: Mon–Sun 10–5.
Closed: Christmas, Boxing and New Year's Days.
Cards: Access, Visa.
Cars: Garden centre car-park.
Toilets: Yes.
Wheelchairs: No steps.
Teas: Available in garden centre. Children's play area.
Mail order: Yes.
Catalogue: Yes. Free.

....

Clearly visible on A5120.
   From M1 exit 12: go north-east towards Flitwick (not Toddington) on the A5120. After 1/2 mile turn right into nursery. The shop is at the rear of the building next to the tearoom.
   From Flitwick: go south towards M1. This nursery is on the left, 1/2 mile before the motorway.

The Factory Shop Guide for East Anglia & South-East England

98 Watford Herts
K Shoes
100 The Parade WD1 5B2
(01923) 243251

Huge selection of K seconds and clearance lines for men, women and children including shoes, sandals, trainers, boots, slippers, handbags.
'All goods are seconds and discontinued lines.'
See display advertisement opposite.

....

In the town centre, inside the inner ring road near Maples and Clements Department Store and opposite Kudos (formerly Paradise Lost) night club.
  Go round the inner road and park in Roslynn Road multi-storey car-park; then walk.

Open: Mon–Sat 9–5.30; most Bank Holidays, but please phone to check.
Closed: Christmas and Boxing Days.
Cards: Access, Visa.
Cars: Local car-parks.
Toilets: Nearby.
Wheelchairs: Easy access to large shop.
Teas: Various places in Watford.
Transport: Local trains and buses.
Mail order: No.

99 Watford Herts
Next 2 Choice
44-46 High Street WD1 2BR
(01923) 233255

Surplus stocks, *Next plc, Next Directory*. Specialising in ladies' and men's wear.
'Save up to 50% off normal Next first quality prices; seconds sold from 1/3 of normal retail price. Special sales Jan & Sept.'

....

Easy to find in the pedestrianised High Street, almost opposite WH Smith and next to Dixons.
  Driving clockwise round the inner ring road: take the right slip-road for Church multi-storey car-park. Go to High Street and turn left, then 300 yds walk and the shop is on left just after Dixons.

Open: Mon–Sat 9–5.30.
Closed: Christmas and Boxing Days.
Cards: Access, Amex, Switch, Visa.
Cars: Car-park in town centre.
Toilets: Church car-park.
Wheelchairs: No steps to large shop.
Changing rooms: No, but refund if returned in perfect condition within 28 days.
Teas: In town centre.
Groups: Shopping groups welcome! Book with store manager.
Transport: Watford BR station .
Mail order: No.

100 Wattisfield Suffolk

Henry Watson's Potteries Ltd.
IP22 1NI
(01359) 251239

Good quality seconds of terracotta storage jars, wine coolers, bread crocks, lasagne dishes, bread bakers, herb and spice jars, flan dishes etc at approximately 25% off; many products at greatly reduced prices. Giftware.

'Lots of bargains, wonderful seconds. Prices from £1.25–£25.'
....

Wattisfield is a small village on the A143, 14 miles north-east of Bury St Edmunds and 9 miles south-west of Diss.
   The Potteries are well signposted: turn up a lane on the right if you come from Bury St Edmunds; turn left if coming from Diss.

Open: Mon–Sat 9.30–4.30; Bank Holidays (except Good Friday).
Closed: Good Friday; Christmas Day and following week.
Cards: Access, Visa.
Cars: Large car-park.
Toilets: Yes, incl. for disabled.
Wheelchairs: No steps to shop, but no easy access for tours.
Teas: Own coffee shop.
Tours: Please phone to book 45-min tour; see an original Roman kiln and factory video. Groups welcome to shop.
Transport: None.
Mail order: No.

The Factory Shop Guide for East Anglia & South-East England

101 Wickford Essex
Next 2 Choice
10–11 Ladygate Centre, High Street SS12 9AK
(01268) 764893

Surplus stocks including men's, women's and children's fashions from *Next plc, Next Directory* and other high street fashions. *Next* footwear.

'Save up to 50% of normal Next first quality prices; seconds sold from 1/3 of normal retail price. Special sales Jan & Sept.'

....

Near southern end of High Street.
From A127: turn onto A132 towards Wickford. Stay on A132 to large roundabout where A129 goes left (and Somerfield is on far left). From this roundabout exit to Somerfield and Ladygate Centre. Shop is in this centre.
From the north on A132: stay on A132 as far as Somerfield on right (by roundabout where A129 turns right for Billericay). Exit this roundabout for Somerfield and Ladygate Centre.

Open: Mon–Thur 9–5.30; Fri 9–6; Sat 9–5.30.
Closed: Christmas and Boxing Days.
Cards: Access, Amex, Switch, Visa.
Cars: In town centre car-park.
Toilets: No.
Wheelchairs: Easy access. No steps.
Changing rooms: No, but refund if returned in perfect condition within 28 days.
Teas: In town centre.
Groups: Shopping groups welcome! Book with store manager.
Transport: Wickford BR station.
Mail order: No.

102 Witham Essex
Hole Farm Dried Flowers
Rivenhall CM8 3HC
(01376) 570434

Pick-your-own flowers for drying. Large range of reasonably priced dried flowers and also some arrangements, ready made and to order. Accessories such as baskets etc. In season, sell PYO strawberries, sweetcorn etc.

'All flowers at lower than usual prices. Buy £30 worth of flowers and get 15% discount.'

....

Just off the A12, about mid-way between Chelmsford and Colchester.
From London/Chelmsford on A12: take the Kelvedon exit; after 300 yds go sharp right and under the A12; the clearly marked farm is on the left.
Coming south-east from Colchester on A12: look for 'Dried Flowers 1 mile' sign; drive slowly in left lane then take left slip road, also signposted. Farm is on left.

Open: Seven days a week, 9–5.
Closed: Please phone to check Christmas openings.
Cards: None.
Cars: Ample parking.
Toilets: Yes.
Wheelchairs: Two shallow steps to small shop.
Teas: Bring your own picnic. Little Chef 1/2 mile.
Tours: Please wander round the farm. Family groups always welcome.
Transport: None.

103 Wrentham Suffolk

Wrentham Basketwear
4–6 London Road NR34 7HF
(01502) 675628

Very wide range of basketware in all shapes and sizes – 320 traditional styles, eg hampers; shopping, bicycle, linen and flower baskets.

'We sell only what we make ourselves. All baskets made from locally grown willow. From £3–£100. Gladly make to commission. See baskets being made.'

....

On the A12, 7 miles south of Lowestoft and 4 miles north of Southwold. Shop is opposite the village hall which is next to large Shell garage.

From Beccles via B1127: go towards Wrentham, pass church on right; take first left; at junction go right on to A12. Shop 100 yds on right.

Open: Mon–Fri 8–5.30; Sat 8–4; Bank Holidays.
Closed: Phone to check Christmas–New Year.
Cards: Access, Visa.
Cars: Small car-park by shop. Ample parking in village.
Toilets: Public toilets 3/4 mile
Wheelchairs: One step to shop, limited space.
Teas: Café next door for teas, snacks, lunches. Pub, restaurant in village.
Tours: Up to 20 people welcome. Please phone 1 week in advance. Meals can be arranged in advance at café next door.
Transport: Bus no. 99 from Lowestoft to Southwold.
Mail order: No.

Postscript from the people who write this book

We hope that this book has brought some pleasure and has made life easier on your pocket. Factory shopping is fun and always carries the air of the unexpected: one never knows what one will find but it is a rare day when one does not find *some*thing irresistible. We visit hundreds of factory shops each year and always enjoy comparing experiences, and bargains, with fellow shoppers whom we meet along the way. There is often a great feeling of camaraderie amongst visitors to a factory shop.

The encouraging letters are absolutely wonderful too and over the years we have developed a close rapport with many readers. Please continue to write!

As regular and loyal readers will already know, the lives of Rolf and myself have revolved around factory shopping for the last nine years. Perhaps 'revolved around' is too gentle a description. More realistically, our lives have been taken over!

Having accidentally discovered our first factory shop in 1985, we began our own personal search for these marvellous money-saving shops and went to a bookshop to buy the relevant guide. Surprised to discover that such shops had never been listed, we published a small book on 40 shops near Nottingham. We were thrilled to find that it sold in its thousands and despite receiving no income that year, we were sufficiently encouraged to keep going with this exhausting research in other areas of the country.

Having been carried away by what started as a part-time hobby, we have visited factory shops in Europe, the US, Hong Kong and Australia, and we follow with interest the new factory outlet centre developments in the UK. Retailing has evolved significantly over the last ten years and we are delighted to find that buying directly from the factory, which had a very low profile when we began, has become the cult form of shopping!

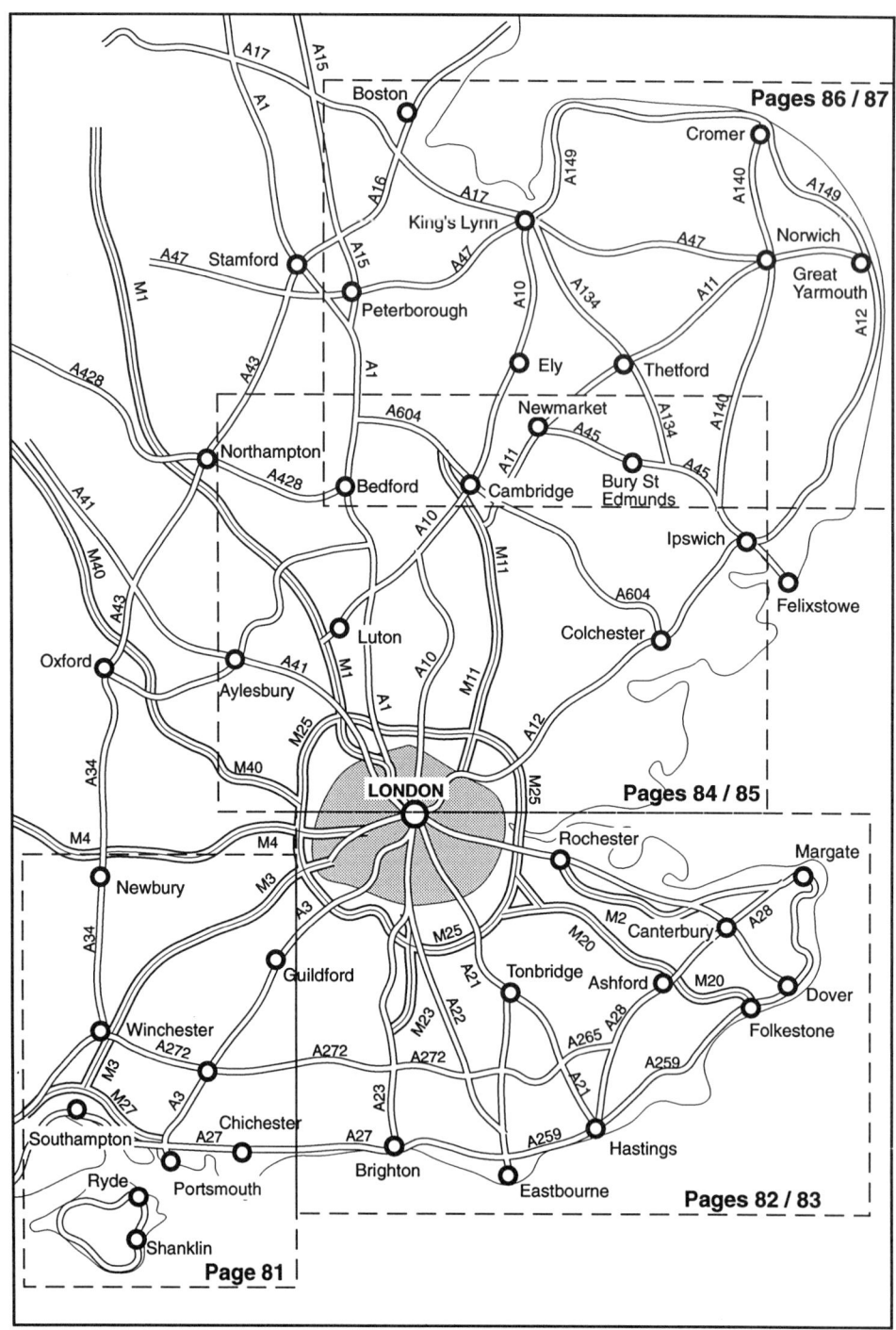

The Factory Shop Guide for East Anglia & South-East England

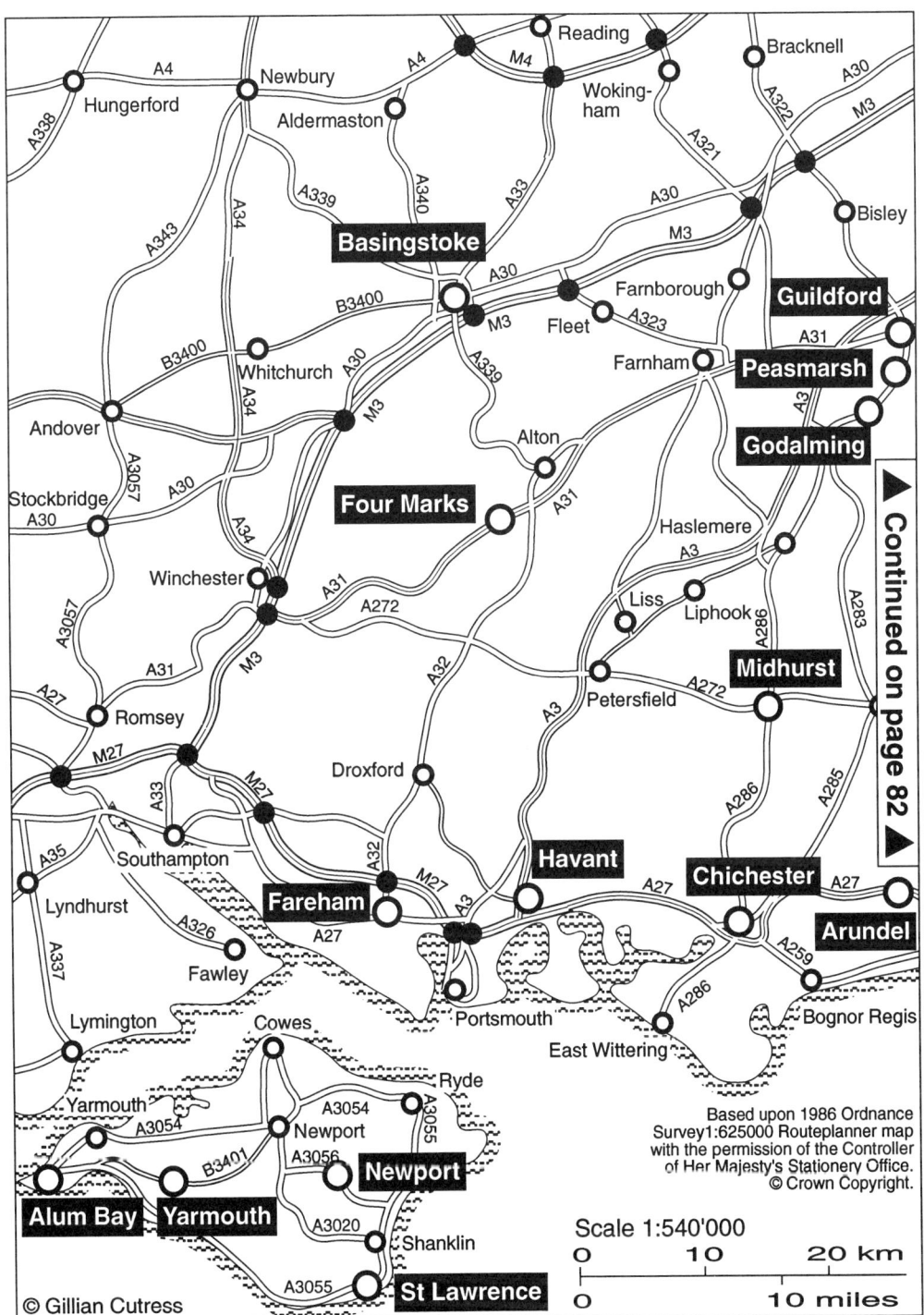

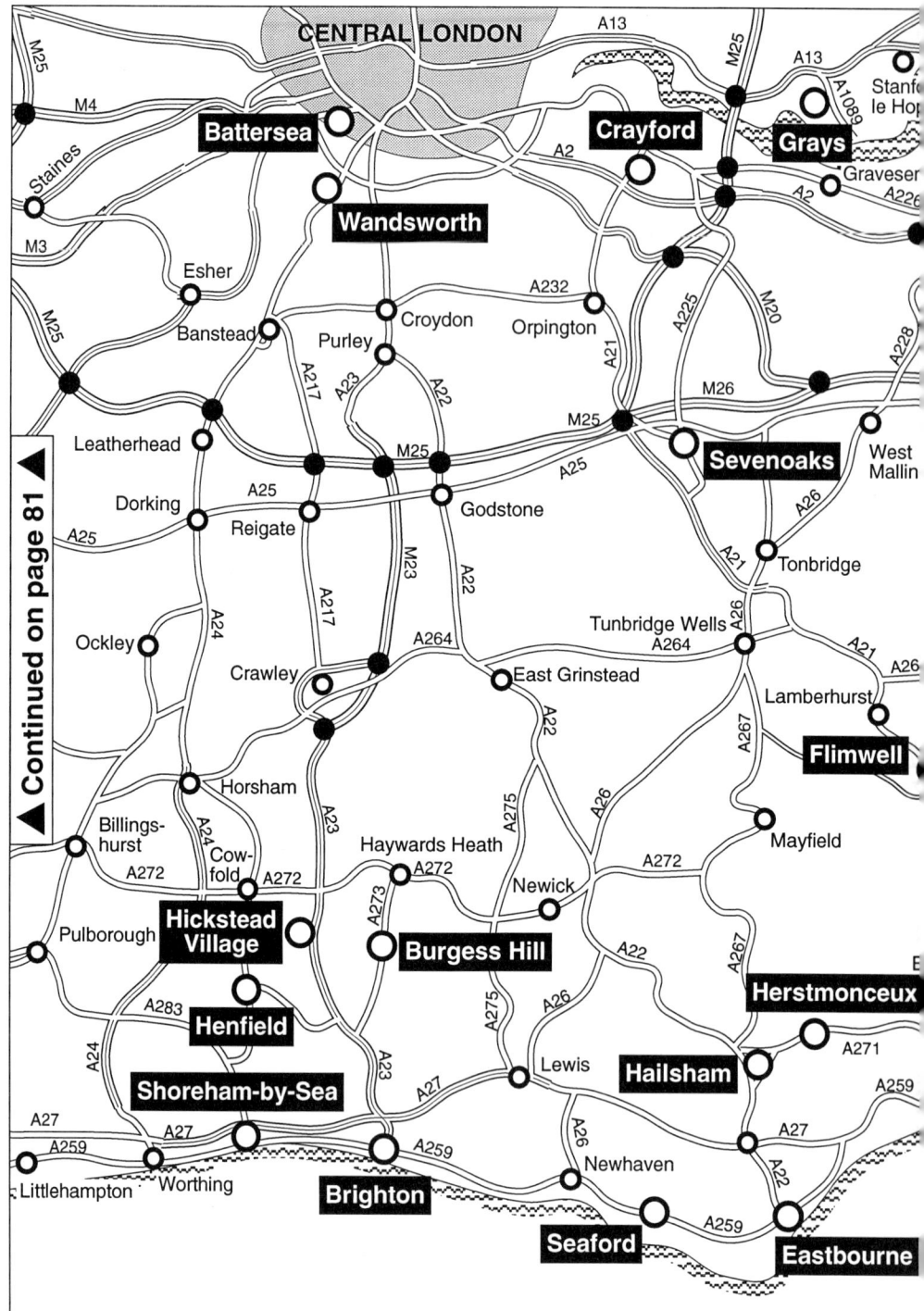

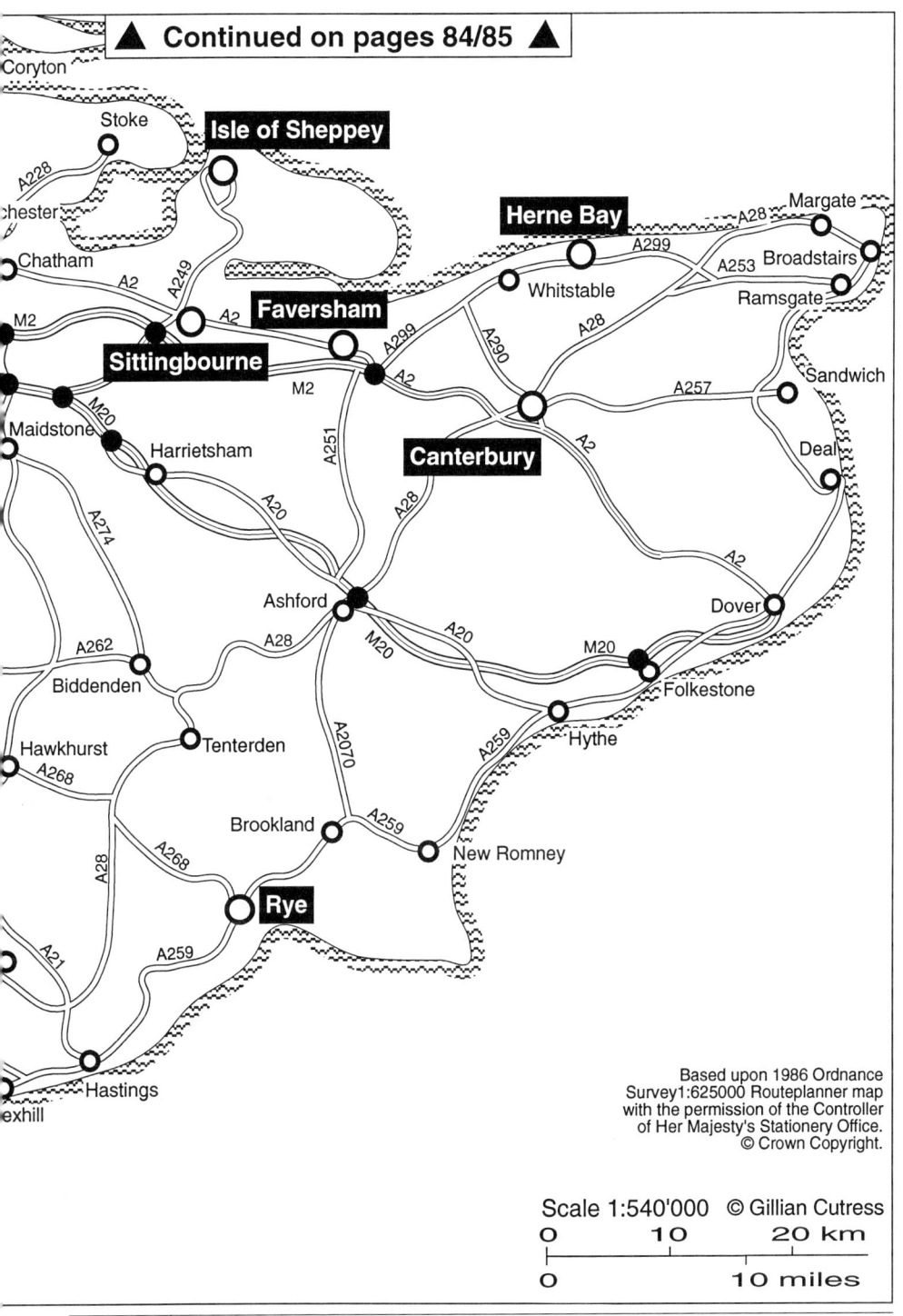

The Factory Shop Guide for East Anglia & South-East England

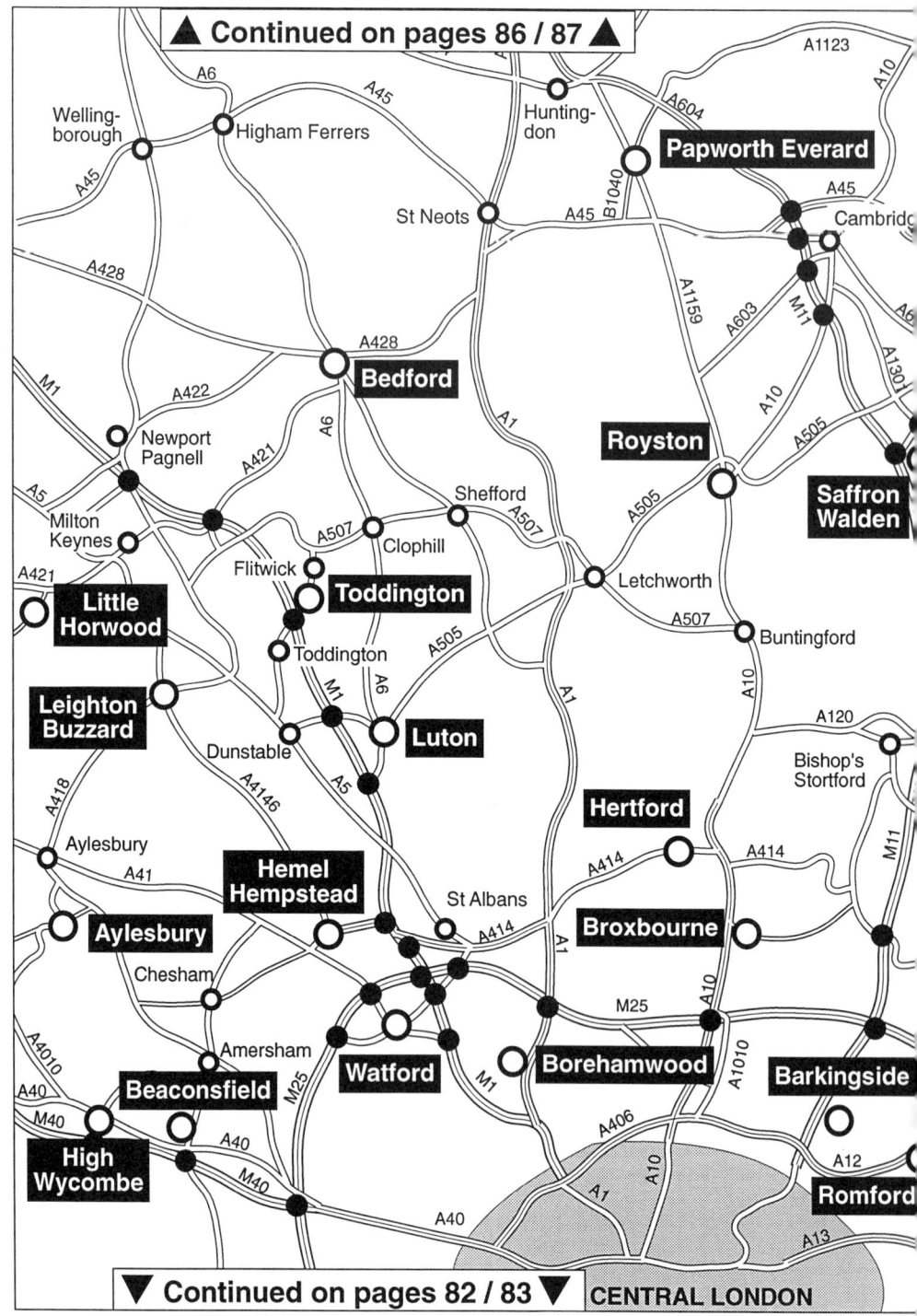

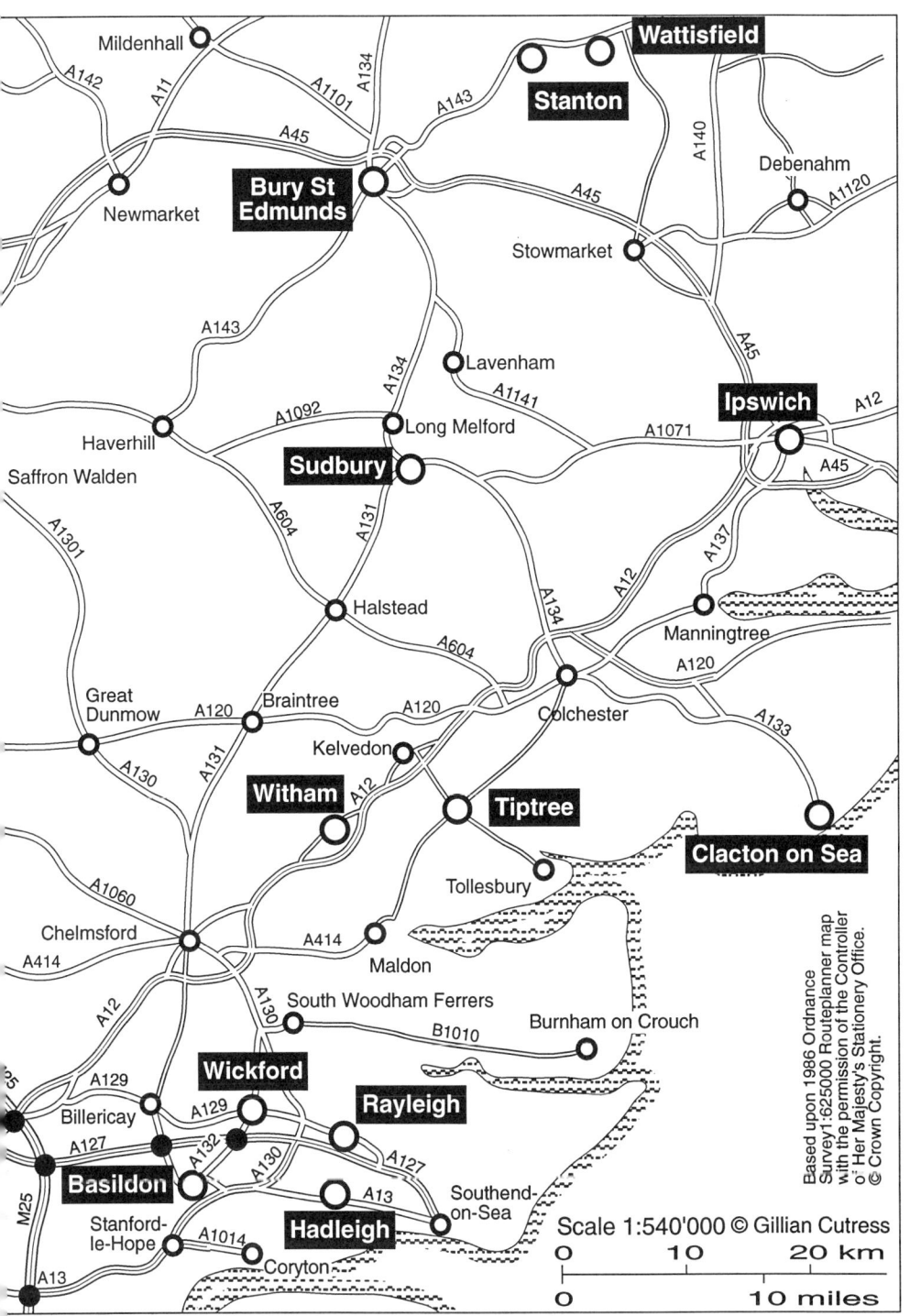

The Factory Shop Guide for East Anglia & South-East England 85

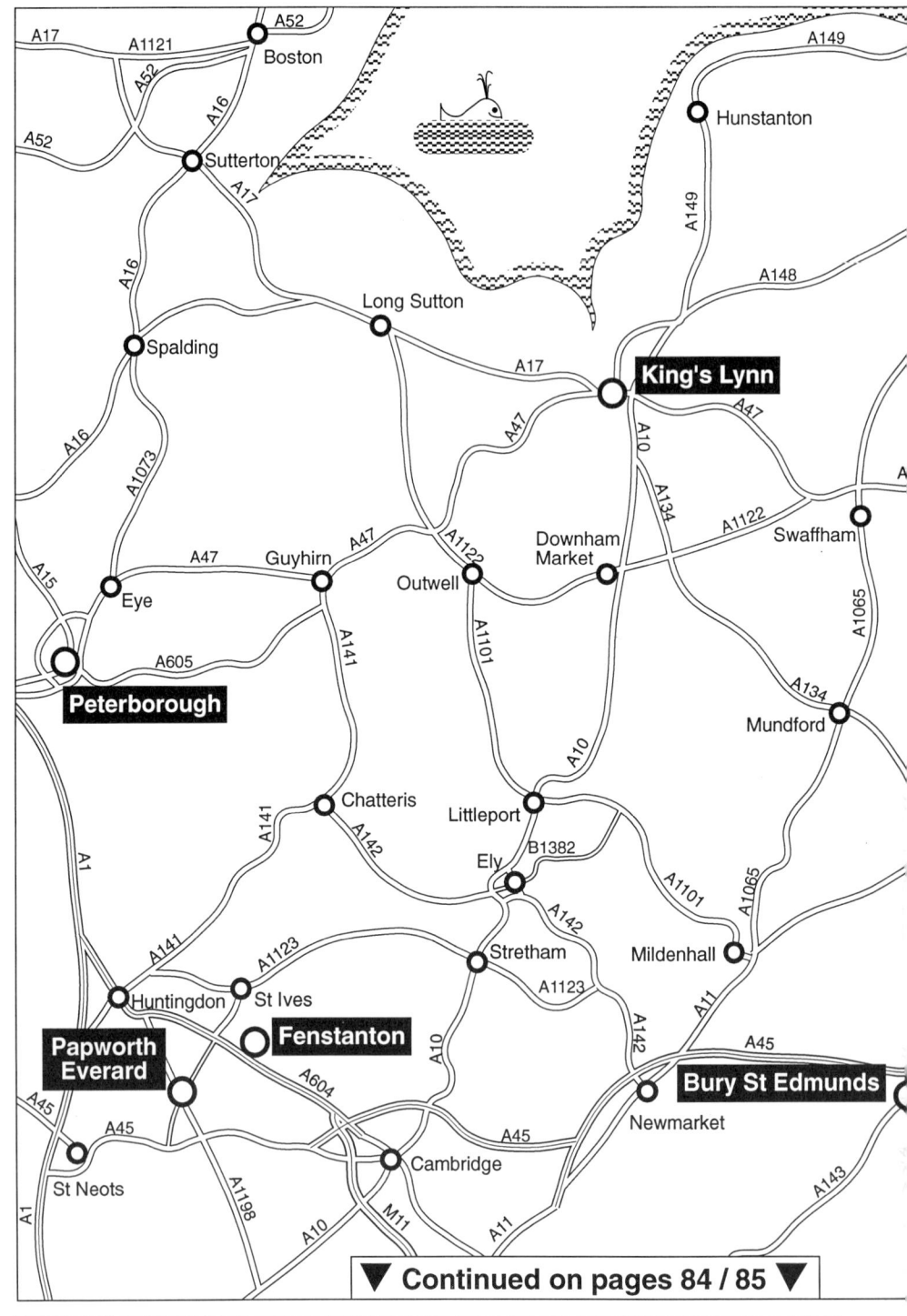

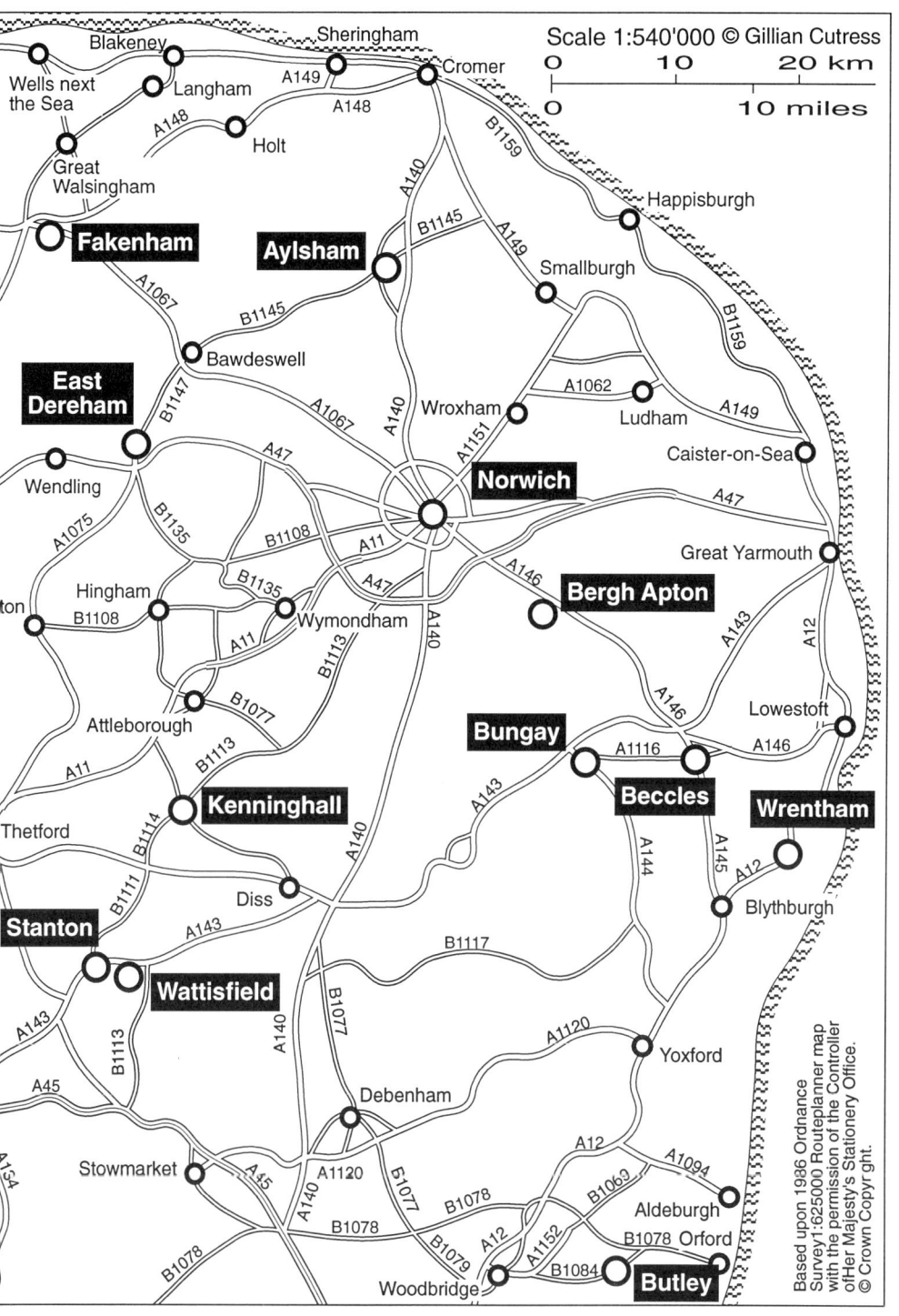

The Factory Shop Guide for East Anglia & South-East England

Other books in The Factory Shop Guide series

SCOTLAND
From John O'Groats to Hadrian's Wall and the Hebrides, very high quality items are on sale: superb cashmere knitwear and international designer woven cashmere; wools and co-ordinated knitwear; tartans and kilts. Buy top quality Scottish jams, soups, shortbread, toffee and boiled sweets. Several super potteries for cookware and animal figurines, cut and engraved crystal glassware, coloured glass paperweights, curtaining, soaps, shiny fashion raincoats, designer sweatshirts, gorgeous sweaters, well known brands of ladies' skirts, jackets & coats, workwear, beds & bedding, garden furniture, terracotta pots, giant casseroles, denim, household linens, sheeting, silk scarves, body-warmers, lightweight raincoats, sheep-skin jackets & good value clothing for all the family. Wick, Lochinver, Ullapool, Inverness, Aberdeen, Oban, Perth, Kinross, Dundee, Stirling, Alva, Dunfermline, Bo'ness, Edinburgh, Kilmarnock, Glasgow, Dunoon, Campbeltown, Ayr, Galashiels, Selkirk, Hawick.

NORTHERN ENGLAND
This part of Britain is rich in shops selling outdoor wear and sports clothes (wetsuits, beachwear, fishing gear, trainers). We tell you how to track down – for the home – beds and mattresses, oven-to-table glass cookware, curtain fabrics, and furniture; to wear – designer silk dresses, men's trousers, underwear, stylish country wear, hats for all occasions and quality leather shoes; plus – an extraordinarily diverse assortment of products including leather brief-cases, lighters, shoe horns, caviar spoons, artists' supplies, Christmas decorations and party poppers. Find well known names in rainwear, clothing, oiled cotton jackets, top quality leather and canvas bags, curtains, a colourful (sweet-smelling) selection of candles, children's clothing, bedding galore, caravan upholstery, stretch car seat covers, carpets, electric tools, crafts materials, fitness shoes, branded leather shoes, vast selections of family footwear, outstanding quality tweeds and hand-woven woollen fabrics, huge ranges of men's jackets, trousers and suits, garden pots and stationery. From Belford and Otterburn south to Washington, Peterlee, Hartlepool, Newcastle, Gateshead, Redcar, Middlesbrough, Stockton, Darlington and Northallerton etc; and Carlisle, Wigton, Maryport, Cleator, Penrith, Keswick, Ambleside, Kendal, the Furness peninsular on the west coast and south to Carnforth.

YORKSHIRE & HUMBERSIDE
96 shops for carpets, towels, blouses, children's and family clothing, furnishing fabrics, sofa beds, skiwear, high quality knitwear, co-ordinated home furnishings, lightweight fleece outdoor clothing, garden furniture and cutlery. Stupendous ranges of knitting yarns (mail order too), footwear, sports wear and men's wear. Humberside has trousers, jackets, chainstore clothing, table lamps, pottery, footwear, leather and sheepskin coats in Bridlington, Driffield, Hull, Immingham, Scunthorpe, Grimsby (for marvellous fresh and smoked fish and Danish specialities). Yorkshire for furnishing fabrics and wallpapers, underwear, shoes, hand-made sprung beds, country furniture, walking breeks, left-handed scissors, cutlery, silver-ware, glassware, linen dishcloths, woollen and worsted fabrics, woollen clothing, tapestry kits, craft materials, pine furniture, tablecloths, hats, gloves, scarves, dress and curtain velvets.

Three factory shop centres. Whitby, York, Ripon, Harrogate, Addingham, Keighley, Skipton, Leeds, Bradford, Hebden Bridge, Halifax, Holmfirth, Huddersfield, Sheffield, Rotherham, Doncaster.

NORTH-WEST ENGLAND

Shops in this area sell great value spectacles, high performance waterproof clothing, famous name high street fashion garments, outstanding selections of curtain fabrics, every possible style in blinds, unusually wide shoes for people who have difficulty in finding comfortable footwear, useful items for the disabled, all styles of lighting, carpets galore, Christmas cards and wrapping paper, and – in two of the most unusual shops we have ever found – Welsh quarry tiles and caviar spoons. This really is an extraordinary area for bedding, curtain and furnishing fabrics and tiles, including famous brand names; if you have not got time or the skill to make the fabric up into curtains, there is no end of people who will do it for you – skilfully and at very reasonable cost. Don't forget the wide range of family clothing, rucksacks, sleeping bags, bedding, knitwear, pond liners, garden equipment, lampshades and bases, small electrical items, toys, sewing threads and a whole host of other wonderful value products. From Lancaster, Blackpool and Runcorn and north Wales including Manchester area and Cheshire.

STAFFORDSHIRE and THE POTTERIES

The ONLY publication that tells you how to find the world-famous potteries – plus some small ones which you have probably not come across before, such as the maker of traditional style Staffordshire dogs. Leading companies such as Portmeirion, Royal Doulton, Aynsley, Spode, Wedgwood are detailed in full. Whether you wish to go around the potteries, to see behind the scenes and watch china being made and decorated, or whether you simply want to find excellent value for money, this book tells you where, when and how. This guide also lets you into the secrets of other companies, with equally famous names, for exquisite enamelled boxes, clothing, wax jackets, hand-cut crystal, country wear, shoes, lingerie and knitwear. From Leek, Biddulph, Kidsgrove to Burton, Lichfield and Tutbury with 39 shops in the Stoke area. Lots of concise maps. Details for overseas visitors on how to get purchases home (that is, which potteries ship purchases, and sales tax information).

THE WESTERN MIDLANDS   (Shropshire; W Mids; Hereford; Worcs; Warks)

Nowhere else will you find such detailed information, along with specially drawn maps, of the traditional hand-cut full lead crystal companies in the Stourbridge area, west of Birmingham. This edition also gives valuable information about the fascinating Jewellery Quarter in Birmingham offering hand-crafted individual jewellery at excellent prices, and skilled repairs. One of the best locations for superb selections of top value-for-money carpets, natural fibre floor coverings, curtains, children's outdoor toys, leather shoes, vibrant hand painted scarves and ties, a vast range of ladies' clothing, trousers, pottery, tableware (Royal Worcester), hair dryers & small electrical items, Christmas tree lights, fitted kitchens, silver plated cutlery & trays etc, brass and copper items, house nameplates, all styles in hats and headwear, designer T-shirts, top branded knitwear, leather items, garden pots, lampshades and lights. Shrewsbury, Craven Arms, Telford, Stourbridge, Stourport, Walsall, Kidderminster, Wolverhampton, Birmingham, Tewkesbury, Worcester, Stratford and Ross on Wye.

DERBYSHIRE, NOTTINGHAMSHIRE & LINCOLNSHIRE

The selection of items is immense, including for the first time shops selling knitwear, lingerie, shoes, underwear, leisurewear, curtains, pottery, terracotta (including finials etc for renovation work), bricks, garden pots, tableware, lace and bridal fabrics, cutlery and an unbelievable range of products previously available from catalogue companies by post. We are delighted to have found new factory shops in Lincolnshire too. Don't forget the famous knitwear, branded jeans, crystal glassware, lace and net curtains, nightwear, lingerie, curtain fabric, picture frames, stylish thermal underwear, children's clothes and large size dresses. Also made-to-measure large sized leisurewear, an immense variety of clothing for all the family and all activities, including fishing and golfing; babywear, luggage, bath cubes and soaps, chocolate, silks, marvellous selections of dress fabrics, cooking & kitchenware, curtains, curtaining, decanters, earthenware, fitted kitchens, fashion shoes, sports shoes & trainers, a broad range of upholstered & leather furniture, garden & terracotta pots, hosiery, lambskin jackets, lightfittings, men's suits, jackets and trousers, paperweights, pillows, safety footwear, shirts, toys, stocking fillers, tablecloths, towels, wallcoverings, Welsh dressers & wrapping paper!

LEICESTERSHIRE, NORTHAMPTONSHIRE & LINCOLNSHIRE

This edition features shops for curtains and curtain fabrics, top quality leather belts and leather items (including golf ball carriers and insulated champagne coolers!), guaranteed reconditioned cookers and kitchen items, co-ordinated bedding, a special range of machine and hand-knitting yarns. You can also buy top value garden urns, columns and statues, lighting and lampshades, soaps and shampoos, internationally renowned duffle coats, family shoes, walking boots, men's hand-made leather footwear, Doc Martens boots, ladies' clothing, boys' underwear, a terrific selection of sports clothing, schoolwear, 100% wool sweaters, carpets, bermuda shorts, men's suits, ladies' jackets, safety footwear, socks and Stilton cheese. Also cosmetics, oven-to-tableware, kitchen and home accessories, handbags, luggage, tablemats, tables and chairs. In Ashby, Shepshed, Coalville, Loughborough, Leicester, Sileby, Wigston, Nuneaton, Oakham; Kettering, Northampton, Wellingborough, Earls Barton; Bedford (for furnishing fabrics).

SOUTH WALES & SOUTH-WEST ENGLAND   incl. the Channel Islands

The latest edition features 105 shops (from Oxfordshire south and west) offering basketware, bedding, clothing for the whole family, carpets, floor and wall tiles, famous cider, garden pots and lots of sheepskin products. Also kitchenware, fitted kitchens, designer silkwear, some fabrics, lots of footwear (incl. made-to-measure for problem feet), safety clothing, furniture, crystal glass, handmade paper, knitwear, lampbases and shades, model animals and houses, a great range of pottery, ribbons, rugs, schoolwear, soft and wooden toys, wools and yarns. From the Channel Islands, through Cornwall and Devon to Gloucestershire (tablemats, carpets, tiles) and Oxfordshire (carpets, pottery, furnishing fabrics); also Christchurch and Poole; Wiltshire (carpets, underwear, table mats, tiles, ladies' clothing); many shops in Somerset, Bristol and 29 shops in South Wales – traditional woollen fabrics, superb cashmere, cakes, boiled sweets, diabetic chocolate, cut glass and full lead crystal wine glasses, household textiles and ladies' quality clothing. See the largest collection of glass marbles in the world!

The Official GREAT BRITISH FACTORY SHOP GUIDE

This new-style guide, esssential for every shrewd shopper, not only gives the when, why, what, how and where of factory shopping but also contains 450 pages and 50 full-page maps with a mass of vital information on 550 factory shops.

We have brought out this new book in response to letters from our readers; we believe that it will be especially useful for visitors and people who tour the UK on business or holiday.

The Official Great British Factory Shop Guide complements our very successful regional books as it is **arranged by product** with 19 chapters on *Clothing, Footwear, Carpets & Floorcoverings, Jewellery, Garden Items, Glass & Cutlery, Electrical Appliances, Pottery, Accessories, Belts, Gloves & Hats, Food & Drink* etc. The shops cover the entire spectrum of items to buy, from top of the market evening wear to serviceable socks for children, from designer bags which are displayed in leading international department stores to plastic holdalls for taking sandwiches to the weekly football match. Details about which companies offer mail order are included for the first time. *The Official Great British Factory Shop Guide* has specially drawn maps, detailed indexes and lots of cross-references.

NORTHERN FRANCE

Cross the Channel & discover a little known shopping trail, or How to make the most of enticing French products at less than traditional French prices!

Our new book, in English and French, is invaluable for shoppers wishing to stretch their francs. This innovative and information-packed guide – the first one of its kind – is ideal for day-trippers and weekenders travelling to France, along with serious Francophiles who have more time in which to seek out the great array of factory shops. You can expect to pay about a third less than normal French prices. From Calais and Boulogne east to St Omer and Lille, over the border into Belgium, then south to Cambrai, Laon, Reims, St Quentin and Troyes, the major factory shopping town in France. Now you can enjoy all those tempting French items with that certain French *je ne sais quoi* – such as outstanding ranges of co-ordinated household linens by leading international names; *Le Creuset* ovenware (seconds can cost as little as a third of the normal UK retail price!); *Cristal d'Arques* tableware; sumptuous *YSL, Daniel Hechter, Descamps, Primrose Bordier* and *Olivier Desforges* designer name bathrobes; exquisite lacy lingerie; *Le Bourget, DD* and *Zanzi* hosiery; stylish women's wear (including *Weill of Paris* and *Paul Mausner*); *Levi's* and *Wrangler* leisurewear; *Le Coq Sportif* and *Adidas* sportswear; *Bally* shoes; ski clothing; hand-made chocolate; traditional French pottery including snail plates!; wonderful continental children's clothes, including *Petit Bateau, Catimini* and *Osh Kosh*; and outstanding men's jackets and suits.

With a total of 234 shops, including four interesting factory outlet centres, this guide gives detailed directions to each shop – with a photo of each. The 'price guide' indicates in advance what you can expect to pay. Champagne trails near Rheims allow you to add a little fizz to your shopping!

You are very welcome to buy these books directly from us – please see the form on p.94

This personally researched guidebook is by a shopping fiend who lives in Milan. As "Italy produces and exports many beautiful luxury goods, be it silks, shoes, furniture or household wares", she has explored the world of seconds, close-outs, showroom models, samples, ends of lines, bargain basements, secondhand shops and artisans. In English and Italian, this invaluable guide (320 pages) gives phone numbers, addresses, and opening hours of 600 places. It is laid out by province (38 shops around Como, 33 in the Florence area, seven near Perugia, 41 entries for Rome, 5 for Bologna, 5 for Verona, 134 in Milan etc). Within each province, the companies are subdivided by product, such as glassware, clothing, jewellery, shoes, gloves, lingerie, lighting, ceramics, fabrics, hosiery, leather ware, silks etc, also with sections on local markets. Examples of prices are given, along with helpful advice such as 'a good address if you want to stock up on fashionable, very wearable costume jewellery at low prices'. Some shops are noted for specially good price/quality/design, some for helpful service.	**Bargain Hunting in Italy** *This "extremely useful guide for the intelligent consumer in search of expensive goods at less expensive prices ..." is available in the UK only from The Factory Shop Guide.* *See the form on p. 94*
Believe it or not, there are 300 factory shops in the Cape Town area. If you are going there on holiday, take advantage of the low Rand. You can find good buys in men's clothing and explore a wide variety of shops selling women's clothing, shoes, sportswear etc. If searching out the shops by yourself seems too daunting, you can join a tour and be guided round the shops by Pam Black, who knows more about South African factory shops than anyone else does. For a free leaflet about Pam's books *The A—Z of Factory Shops* for the Cape area or Natal please send us an SAE. By credit card, you can arrange for a book to be sent to yourself or directly to friends in South Africa. You can also send a voucher (about £13) for a day's shopping with Pam in her small bus – light lunch and wine included!	**Looking for an original and imaginative present for your friends in South Africa?** *Why not send them a Factory Shop Guide for their own country? or give them a present of a day's Factory Shopping Tour?*
We have just discovered that there is a book which tells you how to save money at *Swedish* factory shops! With world-famous names in glass, such as Orrefors, Boda and Kosta Boda and in household articles, Dorre and Scandia – all of which offer items at 30–50% below normal retail prices – this book should soon cover its cost even if you use it just a few times on your Swedish holiday. Clear symbols indicate the type of product manufactured, whether English is spoken, credit cards are accepted and tax free services are offered to tourists (along with essential information on opening times, the availability of toilets, cafés and wheelchair/pram access etc). Basically written in Swedish, it has a useful paragraph in English on how to find each shop and what you can buy; you can quickly see what discount to expect. This varies from shop to shop and on whether you are buying perfect items or seconds. The range of items that you can buy directly from the manufacturer is enormous. Save 40% on your *Primus* stove, for example. Buy Swedish cookware, brassware, decorative wooden items, hand-painted stoneware, porcelain, jewellery, studio glass, harnesses and riding garments, leisurewear, mohair, famous pure wool knitwear, woollen socks, household textiles, linen and lots more. *Available in the UK only from us, £9.95. Please phone for details.*	**Find excellent value-for-money in Sweden too!** *For people who admire Swedish design but who are reluctant to pay traditional Swedish prices, this book will lead them to 170 top value for money shops throughout the country. There is the added bonus of vouchers which give you a further discount of 5–20% in many of the shops!*

Some items on sale in factory shops

Order form

Please send the following books:

..... copy(ies) of **Derbys/Notts/Lincs** at £4.50 each .... £ ......

..... copy(ies) of **Staffordshire & Potteries** at £3.95 .... £ ......

..... copy(ies) of **Yorks/Humberside** Guide at £3.95 each .... £ ......

..... copy(ies) of **Northern England** Guide at £3.95 each .... £ ......

..... copy(ies) of **Leics/Northants/Bedford** at £3.95 each .... £ ......

..... copy(ies) of **Western Midlands** at £3.95 each .... £ ......

..... copy(ies) of **North-West England** at £4.50 each .... £ ......

..... copy(ies) of **Scotland** at £3.95 each .... £ ......

..... copy(ies) of **E Anglia & SE England** at £4.50 each .... £ ......

..... copy(ies) of **SW England & S Wales** at £4.50 each .... £ ......

P&p within UK: 60p for each book, max £3   £ ....

..... copy(ies) of the **Official Great British** Guide at £14.95 .... £ ......

..... copy(ies) of **Northern France** at £9.95 each .... £ ......

..... copy(ies) of the **Italian** Guide at £12.95 each .... £ ......

..... copy(ies) **Gardeners' Atlas (Derbys, Notts, S Yorks)** £6.95 each   £ ......

..... copy(ies) **Gardeners' Atlas (Surrey, SW London, Sussex)** £6.95   £ ......

P&p within UK: £1 for each book, max £3   £ ......

I enclose a cheque / please debit my Visa/Access/Mastercard

Cheques payable to G. Cutress   **FOR OVERALL TOTAL of** £ ......

My name is ....

Address ....

Post Code........................Phone no............................ Date....................

Signed ....

I picked up this leaflet .... (where?)

Please debit my Visa/Access/Mastercard

Number .... Expiry date....................

*OVERSEAS ORDERS: please send your Mastercard or Visa number (plus expiry date)
for airmail delivery (actual postage plus small packing fee).*

To: Gillian Cutress, 1 Rosebery Mews, Rosebery Road, London
SW2 4DQ   phone (0181) 678 0593   fax (0181) 674 1594

Would you like a free book next year?

More manufacturers are opening factory shops. If you have enjoyed visiting other shops, either here, elsewhere in France or Europe, we should be delighted to hear about them. If you are the first person to send us new details which are published next year, we shall be more than happy to send you a free copy of the new Guide.

Name of company ....
Address ....
What do they sell? ....

Name of company ....
Address ....
What do they sell? ....

Name of company ....
Address ....
What do they sell? ....

Name of company ....
Address ....
What do they sell? ....

Where did you buy your copy of the Guide? ....
How did you hear about it? ....

Your Name ....
Your Address ....
....
Town ....
.Post code ....
Your phone no. ....
.Date ....

Readers in Britain only, please send to:
Factory Shop Guide, FREEPOST (SW 8510) London SW2 4BR
(0181) 678 0593   fax (0181) 674 1594

How can we make this Guide even more useful?

To help us provide exactly the information you are looking for, please fill in this questionnaire

Why do you like Factory Shopping?

What don't you like about Factory Shops?

Which shops do you prefer? (please tick only one answer)
a. Shops which sell only those goods they make themselves
b. Shops with a mixture of items, including bought-in goods, relating to this factory
c. Shops which sell anything, including imported items, if they are cheap
d. No preferences
Any other comments?

How much did you spend at the last Factory Shop you visited?
a. Less than £10
b. £10 or more but less than £15
c. £15 or over but less than £20
d. £20 and over but less than £30
e. £30 and over
f. £100 and over

Which items in Factory Shops interest you in particular?
a. Knitting wools
b. Sewing materials
c. Craft materials
d. Pottery & porcelain
e. Glassware
f. Children's clothing
g. Household linens, furnishings
h. General clothing
i. What else?

We are thinking about circulating a newsletter during the year with the latest news about Factory Shops. Please tick if you would like to have further information.

If you are not resident in the area covered by this Guide,
How often each year do you travel to the area?
a. Do you go there on holiday?
b. Do you go there to visit relatives?
c. On holiday and to visit relatives?
d. Other reasons (please specify)
e. For business reasons
f. Specially to visit Factory Shops?

On the day when you last shopped at a Factory Shop, how many individual Factory Shops did you visit in total?

Provided that you have the time, do you enjoy going on a tour of the factory works when you visit a Factory Shop? Very much / it's OK / not much / no thanks
Have you ever been on a coach trip which called in at a Factory Shop? Yes / No
If you have not been on a coach shopping trip, would you like to? Yes / not particularly

Did you buy your own copy of this Guide? Yes / No
Was the book a present? Yes / No   **Have you given a copy to anyone else?** Yes / No

Have you previously bought other Factory Shop Guides? Yes / No   If so, which?

How many of the shops, mentioned in this book, were new to you?
How many people have looked through your copy of this Guide? (include yourself!)
Are you male / female?
Which age bracket are you in? Under 20   20-29   30-39   40-49   50-59   60+
Which paper(s) do you read? Sun Mail Express Telegraph Times Independent Guardian
What other information would you like this Guide to give?   Mirror   Observer   Sun. Times

Any other comments?   Thank you

The Factory Shop Guide for East Anglia & South-East England

Market days

Alton	Tues – outdoor general market.
Ashford	Sat – outdoor general market.
Aylesbury	Wed, Fri, Sat – outdoor general market.
Basildon	Daily except Wed – open general market. Mon flea market.
Basingstoke	Wed, Sat – outdoor general market.
Battle	Tues, Fri – outdoor general market. Sat antiques market.
Bedford	Wed, Sat – outdoor general market.
Braintree	Wed – outdoor general market.
Brighton	Daily – outdoor general markets.
Buckingham	Tues, Sat – outdoor general market.
Burgess Hill	Wed, Sat – outdoor and indoor general markets.
Bury St Edmunds	Wed, Sat – outdoor general market.
Canterbury	Wed – outdoor general market.
Chelmsford	Tues, Fri, Sat – general market. Thur flea market.
Chichester	Wed, Sat – outdoor general market.
Clacton	Tues, Sat – outdoor general market.
Dorking	Fri – general market.
Dover	Daily except Sun – indoor general markets.
Eastbourne	Tues, Fri, Sat – outdoor general markets.
Fakenham	Thur – outdoor general market and flea market.
Fareham	Mon – outdoor general market.
Farnham	Wed – outdoor general market.
Faversham	Tues, Fri, Sat – outdoor general market.
Folkestone	Thur, Sun – outdoor general market.
Godalming	Fri – outdoor general market.
Guildford	Tues, Wed, Thur – outdoor general markets.
Hailsham	Fri – outdoor general market.
Hastings	Daily except Sun – outdoor general markets.
Hemel Hempstead	Thur, Fri, Sat – outdoor general market.
Herne Bay	Sat – outdoor general market.
Hertford	Sat – general outdoor general market.
High Wycombe	Fri, Sat – outdoor general market.
Hove	Thur, Sat, Sun – oudoor general markets. Indoor auction.
Ipswich	Tues, Fri, Sat – outdoor general market.
King's Lynn	Tues, Fri, Sat – outdoor general market.
Leighton Buzzard	Tues, Sat – outdoor general market.
Luton	Mon – Sat – outdoor/indoor general market.
Maidenhead	Daily – outdoor general market.
Milton Keynes	Tues, Sat – outdoor general market.
Norwich	Mon – Sat – outdoor general market.
Peterborough	Tues, Wed, Fri, Sat – outdoor general market.
Romford	Wed, Fri, Sat – outdoor general market.
Rye	Thur – outdoor general market.
Saffron Walden	Tues, Sat – outdoor general market. Sat – indoor general market.
Sevenoaks	Wed – outdoor general market.
Sheerness	Tues, Sat – outdoor general market.
St Albans	Wed – Sat – outdoor general market.
Stowmarket	Thur, Sat – outdoor general market.
Sudbury	Thur, Sat – outdoor general market.
Tonbridge	Sat, Sun – outdoor general markets. Tues, Fri – indoor general mkt.
Tunbridge Wells	Wed, Sat – outdoor general market.
Watford	Tues, Fri, Sat – outdoor general market.
Whitstable	Thur – outdoor general market.

The Factory Shop Guide for East Anglia & South-East England

Towns with factory shops

Please note that the numbers refer to the ENTRIES, NOT the PAGES

Town	No.	Shop
Arundel	1	The Factory Shop
Aylesbury	2	The Chiltern Brewery
Aylsham	3	Black Sheep
Barkingside	4	Choice Discount Stores
Basildon	5	Choice Discount Stores
Basildon	6	The Factory Shop
Basingstoke	7	Western House
Beaconsfield	8	The Curtain Shuffle
Beccles	9	Winter Flora
Bedford	10	Boynett Fabrics
Borehamwood	11	Rubert of London
Brighton	12	Merchant's Quay
Brighton	13	Kemptown Terracotta
Broxbourne	14	Nazeing Glassworks
Bungay	15	Nursey & Son Ltd. (Est. 1790)
Burgess Hill	16	Jaeger Factory Sale Shop
Bury St Edmunds	17	Carpet Bags
Bury St Edmunds	18	The Factory Shop
Butley	19	Butley Pottery
Canterbury	20	Essentially Hops
Chichester	21	Goodwood MetalCraft
Clacton-on-Sea	22	Mascot Clothing
Crayford	23	David Evans and Co.
East Dereham	24	The Factory Shop
Eastbourne	25	Napier
Fakenham	26	Gilchris Confectionery
Fareham	27	Grandford Carpet Mills
Faversham	28	Nova Garden Furniture
Fenstanton near St Ives	29	The Table Place
Flimwell	30	Weald Smokery, The
Four Marks near Alton	31	The Village Furniture Factory
Godalming	32	Alan Paine Knitwear
Godalming	33	Kent & Curwen
Grays	34	Choice Discount Stores
Guildford	35	Susan Walker Classics
Guildford	36	The Wilky Group
Hadleigh	37	Choice Discount Stores
Hailsham	38	The Old Loom Mill
Havant	39	Kenwood
Hemel Hempstead	40	Aquascutum
Henfield	41	Springs Smoked Salmon
Herne Bay	42	Peter Newman
Herstmonceux	43	Thomas Smith's Trug Shop
Hertford	44	Lawthers Factory & Sample Shop
Hickstead Village	45	M & G Designer Fashions
High Wycombe	46	Furniture Direct
High Wycombe	47	GP & J Baker/Parkertex Fabrics
Ipswich	48	Broughton Shoe Warehouse
Ipswich	49	Lambourne Clothing
Isle of Wight : Yarmouth	50	Chessell Pottery
Isle of Wight : Alum Bay	51	Alum Bay Glass
Isle of Wight : Newport	52	Haseley Manor & Pottery

Towns with factory shops contd.

Please note that the numbers refer to the ENTRIES, NOT the PAGES

Town	Entry	Shop
Isle of Wight : St Lawrence	53	Isle of Wight Glass
Kenninghall	54	Suffolk Potteries
King's Lynn	55	Caithness Crystal
King's Lynn	56	Jaeger
King's Lynn	57	Start-rite Shoes
Leighton Buzzard	58	Gossard
Little Horwood	59	Phoenix Carpets
London : Balham	60	Indian Ocean Trading Company
London : Battersea	61	Price's Patent Candle Co
London : Bow	62	Nicole Farhi/French Connection
London : Bromley-by-Bow	63	Furniture Mill, The
London : Ealing	64	Corcoran & May
London : East Ham	65	Paul Simon Furnishings
London : Fulham	66	Roger Lascelles Clocks
London : Hackney	67	Hanging Garments (Burberrys)
London : Hackney	68	The Factory Shop (Sofa to Bed)
London : Leyton	69	R P Ellen
London : Putney	70	Corcoran & May
London : Wandsworth	71	In-Wear
London : Wandsworth	72	Villeroy & Boch
London : West Norwood	73	W Hobby
Luton	74	Kangol
Midhurst	75	Dexam International
Norwich	76	Bally Factory Shop, The
Norwich	77	Country House Flowers
Norwich	78	Factory Shoe Shop, The
Norwich	79	Robert Cole Shoes
Papworth Everard	80	Papworth Travel Goods
Peterborough	81	Jaeger Sale Shop
Peterborough	82	Stage 2 (Freemans)
Rayleigh	83	Falmer Jeans
Romford	84	Hubbinet Reproductions
Royston	85	The Shoe Shed
Rye	86	Rye Pottery
Saffron Walden	87	Swaine Adeney Brigg
Seaford	88	Sheban Furniture
Sevenoaks	89	Corcoran & May
Sheerness, Isle of Sheppey	90	B & A Whelan
Shoreham-by-Sea	91	Claremont Garments
Sittingbourne	92	Michelsons
Slough	93	Mexx Factory Outlet
Stanton nr Bury St Edmunds	94	Playdri Products
Sudbury	95	Vanners Mill Shop
Tiptree	96	The Factory Shop
Toddington	97	Royal Scot Crystal
Watford	98	K Shoes
Watford	99	Next 2 Choice
Wattisfield	100	Henry Watson's Potteries
Wickford	101	Next 2 Choice
Witham	102	Hole Farm Dried Flowers
Wrentham	103	Wrentham Basketwear

Companies with factory shops

Please note that the numbers refer to the ENTRIES, NOT the PAGES

Alan Paine Knitwear... 32	Godalming
Alum Bay Glass... 51	Isle of Wight : Alum Bay
Aquascutum... 40	Hemel Hempstead
Baker, GP & J/Parkertex Fabrics.... 47	High Wycombe
Bally Factory Shop, The... 76	Norwich
Black Sheep...... 3	Aylsham
Boynett Fabrics... 10	Bedford
Broughton Shoe Warehouse... 48	Ipswich
Butley Pottery... 19	Butley
Caithness Crystal... 55	King's Lynn
Carpet Bags... 17	Bury St Edmunds
Chessell Pottery.... 50	Isle of Wight : Yarmouth
Chiltern Brewery, The..... 2	Aylesbury
Choice Discount Stores..... 4	Barkingside
Choice Discount Stores..... 5	Basildon
Choice Discount Stores... 34	Grays
Choice Discount Stores... 37	Hadleigh
Claremont Garments... 91	Shoreham-by-Sea
Corcoran & May... 64	London : Ealing
Corcoran & May .. 70	London : Putney
Corcoran & May... 89	Sevenoaks
Country House Flowers... 77	Norwich
Curtain Shuffle, The..... 8	Beaconsfield
David Evans... 23	Crayford
Dexam International... 75	Midhurst
Ellen, R P... 69	London : Leyton
Essentially Hops... 20	Canterbury
Factory Shoe Shop, The... 78	Norwich
Factory Shop, The..... 1	Arundel
Factory Shop, The..... 6	Basildon
Factory Shop, The... 18	Bury St Edmunds
Factory Shop, The... 24	East Dereham
Factory Shop, The... 96	Tiptree
Factory Shop, The (Sofa to Bed) 68	London : Hackney
Falmer Jeans... 83	Rayleigh
Furniture Direct... 46	High Wycombe
Furniture Mill... 63	London : Bromley-by-Bow
Gilchris Confectionery... 26	Fakenham
Giltpack Engineering... 94	Southampton
Goodwood MetalCraft... 21	Chichester
Gossard... 58	Leighton Buzzard
Grandford Carpet Mills... 27	Fareham
Hanging Garments (Burberrys)... 67	London : Hackney
Haseley Manor & Pottery... 52	Isle of Wight : Newport
Henry Watson's Potteries. 100	Wattisfield
Hobby, W 73	London : West Norwood
Hole Farm Dried Flowers. 102	Witham
Hubbinet Reproductions... 84	Romford
In-Wear... 71	London : Wandsworth
Indian Ocean Trading Company... 60	London : Balham
Isle of Wight Glass... 53	Isle of Wight : St Lawrence
Jaeger... 56	King's Lynn

100   The Factory Shop Guide for East Anglia & South-East England

Companies with factory shops *contd.*

Please note that the numbers refer to the ENTRIES, NOT the PAGES

Jaeger...	16	Burgess Hill
Jaeger...	81	Peterborough
K Shoes...	98	Watford
Kangol....	74	Luton
Kemptown Terracotta...	13	Brighton
Kent & Curwen...	33	Godalming
Kenwood...	39	Havant
Lambourne Clothing...	49	Ipswich
Lawthers Factory & Sample Shop...	44	Hertford
M & G Designer Fashions...	45	Hickstead
Mascot Clothing...	22	Clacton-on-Sea
Merchants Quay...	12	Brighton
Mexx...	93	Slough
Michelsons...	92	Sittingbourne
Napier...	25	Eastbourne
Nazeing Glassworks...	14	Broxbourne
Next 2 Choice...	99	Watford
Next 2 Choice.	101	Wickford
Nicole Farhi/French Connection...	62	London : Bow
Nova Garden Furniture...	28	Faversham
Nursey & Son...	15	Bungay
Old Loom Mill, The...	38	Hailsham
Papworth Travel Goods...	80	Papworth Everard
Paul Simon Furnishings...	65	London : East Ham
Peter Newman...	42	Herne Bay
Phoenix Carpets...	59	Little Horwood
Playdri Products...	94	Stanton (Bury St Edmunds)
Price's Patent Candle...	61	London : Battersea
Robert Cole Shoes...	79	Norwich
Roger Lascelles Clocks...	66	London : Fulham
Royal Scot Crystal...	97	Toddington
Rubert of London...	11	Borehamwood
Rye Pottery...	86	Rye
Sheban Furniture...	88	Seaford
Shoe Shed, The...	85	Royston
Springs Smoked Salmon...	41	Henfield
Stage 2 (Freemans)...	82	Peterborough
Start-rite Shoes...	57	King's Lynn
Suffolk Potteries...	54	Kenninghall
Susan Walker Classics...	35	Guildford
Swaine Adeney Brigg...	87	Saffron Walden
Table Place, The...	29	Fenstanton near St Ives
Thomas Smith's Trug Shop...	43	Herstmonceux
Vanners...	95	Sudbury
Village Furniture Factory, The...	31	Four Marks near Alton
Villeroy & Boch...	72	London : Wandsworth
Weald Smokery, The...	30	Flimwell
Western House.....	7	Basingstoke
Whelan, B & A...	90	Sheerness, Isle of Sheppey
Wilky Group...	36	Guildford
Winter Flora.....	9	Beccles
Wrentham Basketwear.	103	Wrentham

The Factory Shop Guide for East Anglia & South-East England 101

Index

Please note that the numbers refer to the ENTRIES, NOT the PAGES

Animal sculptures & figurines	21, 50, 75, 86
Bags, cases & luggage	12, 17, 18, 78, 80, 96, 98
Baskets	43, 103
Bathroom suites	36
Bedding	12, 18, 24, 82, 96
Beds	46, 68
Beer, barley wine, cider	2
Biscuits	26
Briefcases	80
Candles	61
Carpets & rugs	27, 59
Cashmere clothing, knitwear & accessories	32, 35
Catalogue goods	4, 5, 34, 37, 82, 99, 101
China & porcelain	6, 7, 13, 21, 50, 52, 54, 72, 75, 86, 100
Chocolate	26
Clocks	66
Clothing	
baby & children's	91
evening & occasion	11, 44, 45
for all the family	3, 4, 5, 6, 12, 18, 24, 34, 37, 71, 82, 83, 91, 93, 96, 99, 101
knitwear	3, 16, 32, 35, 40, 49, 56, 62, 67, 81
ladies'	11, 16, 17, 22, 32, 35, 40, 44, 45, 49, 56, 58, 62, 67, 71, 74, 81, 82, 87, 92
large sizes	11, 45
leather	15
lingerie	58, 91
men's	16, 17, 22, 32, 33, 35, 40, 49, 56, 67, 81, 82, 87, 92
outdoor, climbing, walking	3, 22, 67, 87, 94
rainwear	11, 40, 44, 67
silk	23, 95
sports	1, 94
woollen	3, 32, 35
Company promotional items	92
Confectionery	26
Cooking & kitchen ware	21, 75, 100
Corsetry	58
Cosmetics	24
Costume jewellery	25
Countrywear	3, 22, 87
Courses	19, 77
Craft materials	73
Cricket clothing	1, 33
Croquet sets	60
Curtain-making service	10, 46, 64, 65, 70, 89
Curtaining	4, 5, 10, 37, 38, 47, 64, 65, 70, 89
Curtains	4, 5, 8, 10, 37, 64, 65, 70, 89
Dolls' houses	73
Dried flowers & arrangements	9, 20, 77, 102
Earrings	25
Earthenware	52, 86
Electrical items	39
Fabrics	
curtaining	4, 5, 10, 37, 38, 47, 64, 65, 70, 89
dress	23, 38, 95
furnishing	10, 38, 47, 64, 65, 70, 89
silk	23, 95
Factory tours & demonstrations	2, 9, 13, 14, 19, 20, 23, 43, 50, 51, 52, 53, 54, 55, 61, 63, 65, 66, 92, 100, 102

The Factory Shop Guide for East Anglia & South-East England

Index contd.

Please note that the numbers refer to the ENTRIES, NOT the PAGES

Fashion jewellery	25
Fish	30, 41
Floor & wall tiles	13
Floor covering, carpets and rugs	27, 59
Food & drink	2, 26, 30, 41
Food smoked	30, 41
Footwear	4, 5, 12, 24, 34, 37, 37, 42, 48, 57, 69, 76, 78, 79, 85, 96, 98, 101
Fountains & birdbaths	90
Furniture	
beds	46, 68
cane	24, 28
garden	6, 28, 60
period-style	29, 31, 63, 84, 88
pine	24
rustic	43
teak	60
upholstered	10, 24, 46, 68
wooden	29, 31, 63, 84, 88
Garden pots & ornaments	13, 54, 90
Garden trugs	43
Glassware & crystal	7, 12, 14, 51, 53, 55, 72, 97
Gloves mittens hats & scarves	15
Gnomes for the garden	90
Golfwear & other items	1, 33, 94
Greetings cards	6
Handbags	76, 78, 98
Handbasins	36
Hats	74
Hop bines	20
Household linens & textiles	6, 24, 96
Irons	39
Jeans	71, 83, 93
Jewellery	25, 51
Kettles	39
Kitchen & home accessories	6, 39, 54, 100
Knitwear	3, 16, 32, 33, 35, 40, 49, 56, 62, 67, 81
Lampshades & bases	18, 96
Lavatory pans	36
Leather items	15
Leather travel goods	80
Leatherwear	15
Lingerie	58, 91
Luggage	17, 80, 96
Mail order surplus	4, 5, 34, 37, 82, 99, 101
Majolica	19
Marzipan	26
Model kits	73
Museum	2, 23
Nightwear	91
Outerwear	3, 15, 22, 67, 87, 94
Paperweights	14, 51, 53, 55, 97
Patio & conservatory furniture	28, 60
Period-style furniture	29, 31, 63, 84, 88
Pick your own flowers	77, 102
Picnic hampers	103
Pine furniture	24

The Factory Shop Guide for East Anglia & South-East England

Index contd.

Please note that the numbers refer to the ENTRIES, NOT the PAGES

Pottery	6, 7, 13, 19, 21, 50, 52, 54, 72, 75, 86, 100
Rainwear	11, 40, 44, 67
Reproduction furniture	29, 31, 63, 84, 88
Roof tiles	13
Rugs & carpets	27, 59
Rustic furniture	43
Seafood	30, 41
Sheepskin clothing & accessories	15
Sheets, pillows & quilts	12, 18, 24, 82, 96
Shoes	
children's	57
for all the family	4, 5, 12, 18, 24, 34, 37, 42, 48, 76, 79, 85, 96, 98, 101
golf & bowls	94
ladies'	69, 76, 78
leather	69, 76
men's	76, 78
wide fittings	78
Silk accessories	23, 92, 95
Silk fabric	23, 95
Silver plated items	7
Smoked fish	30, 41
Soaps and toiletries	18, 24
Sofa beds	46, 68
Speciality foods	2, 30, 41
Sports, casual & leisurewear	1, 12, 33, 71, 83, 94
Stainless steel items	21, 75
Stationery	6
Studio glass	51, 53
Suits, jackets & trousers	11, 16, 33, 44, 45, 45, 56, 67, 81
Sweets	26
Tables & chairs	28, 29, 31, 60, 63
Tableware	
pottery	7, 19, 52, 72
stainless steel	21, 75
Tapestry bags	17
Taps	36
Terracotta	13, 54, 100
Ties	23, 33, 92, 95
Tiles	13
Toasters	39
Tools	73
Towels	6, 24
Toy making kits	73
Toys	6, 82
Travel goods	80
Trenchcoats	67
Trugs	43
Underwear	58, 91
Upholstered furniture	10, 24, 46, 68
Wallpaper	47
Waterproofs	22, 87, 94
Waxed jackets	15, 22, 67, 87, 94
Wooden furniture	29, 31, 60, 63, 84, 88
Woollen items, caps gloves shawls scarves	3
Wools & yarns	38